The Structure and Practices of the
Debt Buying Industry

REPORT CONTRIBUTORS

BUREAU OF CONSUMER PROTECTION

Thomas Kane, Attorney, Division of Financial Practices

Jason Schall, Attorney, Division of Financial Practices

Heather Allen, Attorney, Division of Financial Practices

Daniel Dwyer, Attorney, Division of Financial Practices

Bevin Murphy, Attorney, Northeast Region

Thomas Pahl, Assistant Director, Division of Financial Practices

Jessica Rich, Associate Director, Division of Financial Practices

Jose Oyola-Sepulveda, Paralegal, Division of Financial Practices

TJ Peeler, Visual Information Specialist, Division of Consumer and Business Education

BUREAU OF ECONOMICS

Daniel Becker, Economist, Division of Consumer Protection

Marc Luppino, Economist, Division of Consumer Protection

Margaret Patterson, Economist, Division of Consumer Protection

James Lacko, Deputy Assistant Director, Division of Consumer Protection

Janis Pappalardo, Assistant Director, Division of Consumer Protection

Ania Jaroszewicz, Research Analyst, Bureau of Economics

Benjamin Miller, Research Analyst, Bureau of Economics

Julie Miller, Research Analyst, Bureau of Economics

John Mountjoy, Research Analyst, Bureau of Economics

Joseph Remy, Research Analyst, Bureau of Economics

Eric Shaeffer, Research Analyst, Bureau of Economics

Michael Shores, Research Analyst, Bureau of Economics

Scott Syms, Research Analyst, Bureau of Economics

Aleksey Verkhivker, Research Analyst, Bureau of Economics

CONTENTS

EXECUTIVE SUMMARY

In a 2009 study of the debt collection industry, the Commission concluded that the "most significant change in the debt collection business in recent years has been the advent and growth of debt buying." "Debt buying" refers to the sale of debt by creditors or other debt owners to buyers that then attempt to collect the debt or sell it to other buyers. Debt buying can reduce the losses that creditors incur in providing credit, thereby allowing creditors to provide more credit at lower prices. Debt buying, however, also may raise significant consumer protection concerns.

The FTC receives more consumer complaints about debt collectors, including debt buyers, than about any other single industry. Many of these complaints appear to have their origins in the quantity and quality of information that collectors have about debts. In its 2009 study, the Commission expressed concern that debt collectors, including debt buyers, may have insufficient or inaccurate information when they collect on debts, which may result in collectors seeking to recover from the wrong consumer or recover the wrong amount.

The FTC initiated this debt buyer study in late 2009 for two main purposes. First, the FTC sought to obtain a better understanding of the debt buying market and the process of buying and selling debt. Second, the Commission wanted to explore the nature and extent of the relationship, if any, between the practice of debt buying and the types of information problems that the FTC has found can occur when debt collectors seek to recover and verify debts.

Many stakeholders recognize the concerns that have been raised about debt buying, including consumer groups, members of Congress, federal and state regulatory and enforcement agencies, and the debt buyer industry itself. Indeed, the debt buyer industry has launched a self-regulatory effort to address some of these concerns, and the FTC is encouraged by that effort. This study of debt buyers is the first large-scale empirical assessment of the debt buying sector of the collection industry. The FTC hopes that its findings contribute to a greater understanding of debt buying, enhance ongoing reform efforts, and prompt further study of the industry.

STUDY OVERVIEW

To conduct its study, the Commission obtained information about debts and debt buying practices from nine of the largest debt buyers that collectively bought 76.1% of the debt sold in 2008, with six of these debt buyers providing the information the Commission used in most of its analysis. The FTC also considered its prior enforcement and policy work related to debt collection, as well as available research concerning debt buying. The study focused on large debt buyers because they account for most of the debt purchased; it did not address the practices of smaller debt buyers that are a frequent source of consumer protection concerns, a limitation that must be considered in evaluating the study's findings.

The Commission acquired and analyzed an unprecedented amount of data from the studied debt buyers, which submitted data on more than 5,000 portfolios, containing nearly 90 million consumer accounts, purchased during the three-year study period. These accounts had a face value of $143 billion, and the debt buyers spent nearly $6.5 billion to acquire them. Most portfolios for which debt buyers submitted data were credit card debt, with such debt accounting for 62% of all portfolios and 71% of the total amount that the buyers spent to acquire debts. In addition to these data, the debt buyers provided copies of many purchase and sale agreements between themselves and sellers of debts. The debt buyers also submitted narrative responses to questions concerning their companies and their practices, as well as the debt buying industry.

The key findings of the study are as follows:

PRICES BUYERS PAID FOR PURCHASED DEBT

Buyers paid an average of 4.0 cents per dollar of debt face value. Analysis of the prices debt buyers paid for debt purchased in more than 3,400 portfolios showed that the average price was 4.0 cents per dollar of debt face value. Older debt sold for a significantly lower price than newer debt. The price of debt older than 15 years was virtually zero. Buyers paid similar prices for debt purchased from original creditors and resellers, once the analysis controlled for other observable characteristics of the debt, such as their age and type.

INFORMATION THAT DEBT BUYERS RECEIVED

Buyers typically received the information required for validation notices. Buyers were likely to have received from sellers the information that the FDCPA currently requires that debt collectors include with validation notices at the beginning of the collection process, including the amount of the debt. They also either received or were likely aware of the name of the original creditor, which the FDCPA requires that they provide to consumers upon written request.

Buyers also typically received additional information that could make validation notices more useful, but they usually did not provide it to consumers. Buyers also typically received additional information that, if disclosed to consumers, might help consumers assess whether they are the correct debtor and whether the amount of the debt is correct. This information included the name of the original creditor, the original creditor's account number, the debtor's social security number, the date of last payment, and the date of charge-off. In the Commission's experience, however, debt collectors, including debt buyers, generally do not include these types of additional information in their validation notices.

Buyers rarely received dispute history. Buyers rarely received any information from sellers concerning whether a consumer had disputed the debt or whether the disputed debt had been verified – information that would bear on whether the consumer being contacted owes the debt and whether the amount being collected is correct. Moreover, buyers often did not receive information that would allow them to break down the outstanding balance into principal, interest, and fees. The Commission has found that such information would assist consumers in determining if the amount of their debts is correct.

ACCOUNT DOCUMENTATION THAT DEBT BUYERS RECEIVED

Buyers received few underlying documents about debts. Although buyers received the data file and some other information about the debts, as discussed above, they obtained very few documents related to the purchased debts at the time of sale or after purchase. For most portfolios, buyers did not receive any documents at the time of purchase. Only a small percentage of portfolios included documents, such as account statements or the terms and conditions of credit.

WARRANTIES AS TO INFORMATION AND DOCUMENTATION THAT DEBT BUYERS RECEIVED

Accuracy of information provided about debts at time of sale not guaranteed. In purchase and sale agreements obtained in the study, sellers generally disclaimed all representations and warranties with regard to the accuracy of the information they provided at the time of sale about individual debts – essentially selling debts, with some limited exceptions, "as is." The fact that portfolios were generally sold "as is" does not necessarily mean that information inaccuracies were prevalent, but it does raise concerns about how debt buyers handled purchased debts when such inaccuracies became apparent, and for which they had no recourse available from the seller.

Accuracy of information in sellers' documents not guaranteed. Some contracts stated that when account documents were available from the seller, the accuracy of the information in the documents was not warranted.

DEBT BUYERS' ABILITY TO OBTAIN ACCOUNT DOCUMENTATION

Limitations were placed on debt buyer access to account documents. Buyers were given a defined amount of time (*e.g.*, typically between six months and three years) to request up to a specified maximum number of documents (*e.g.*, equal to 10% to 25% of the number of debts in the portfolio) at no charge. After that, buyers were given an additional, defined amount of time to request documents for a fee, usually between $5 and $10 per document, with a maximum number of documents again specified. Debt sellers usually had substantial time, typically between 30 and 60 days, to respond to requests for documents.

Availability of documents not guaranteed. Most purchase and sale agreements stated that documents may not be available for all accounts.

Additional limitations applied to the resale of purchased debt. If debt buyers resold debt to secondary buyers, the original creditors typically had no obligation to provide documents directly to the secondary buyers; instead the secondary buyers were required to forward document requests through the original buyers, which sometimes added additional fees and delays.

Consumers disputed 3.2% of debts that buyers attempted to collect themselves. The data obtained in the study from the four debt buyers that submitted information on written and some oral disputes showed that consumers disputed 3.2% of the debts that debt buyers attempted to collect themselves. (The Commission did not obtain information on disputes of debts for which buyers hired third-party collectors to recover for them). There was no statistically significant relationship between the likelihood of a dispute and a debt's age, face value, or whether it had been purchased from an original creditor or reseller.

Consumers disputed an estimated one million debts each year. Although the 3.2% dispute rate may understate the extent of information problems in purchased debt, even a 3.2% dispute rate, if applied to the entire debt buying industry, indicates that each year buyers sought to collect about one million debts that consumers asserted they did not owe. The proper handling of this large number of disputed debts is a significant consumer protection concern.

About half of disputed debts were reported as verified. Buyers reported that they had verified 51.3% of the debts consumers disputed. Older debt was less likely to be verified. The Commission did not examine what buyers did to verify debts or whether the verification was adequate. Similarly, for the debts that had not been verified, the Commission did not have information to determine whether buyers attempted to verify the debts but could not, or whether they simply did not attempt verification. If this verification rate is applied to the one million debts estimated to have been disputed in the debt buying industry each year, it would indicate that each year about 500,000 disputed debts were not verified by buyers.

Few disputed debts were resold. Debt buyers in the study sold only 2.9% of their disputed debts, including 4.9% of verified disputed debts and 0.8% of unverified disputed debts. The FDCPA prohibits debt collectors, including debt buyers, from seeking to recover on unverified disputed debt, but it does not bar them from reselling such debts to other purchasers, or bar subsequent purchasers from seeking to collect the debt. Such sales, however, likely contribute to collectors seeking to recover from the wrong consumer or the wrong amount.

Some debt was beyond the statute of limitations, though most was not. Many states have statute of limitations barring lawsuits to collect on a debt after a certain period, typically between three and six years for credit card debts. Although the debt buyers studied purchased and collected on debts that were more than six years old, most of the debt that they purchased did not appear to be either old or beyond the statute of limitations. This finding, however, may not be applicable to the debts that smaller debt buyers not included in the study purchased.

Debt buyers generally know the ages of debts they are collecting. Information provided to debt buyers with the purchased debt generally included the age of the debt.

I. INTRODUCTION

In recent years, a significant focus of the FTC's research and policy work has been identifying and addressing consumer protection problems relating to debt collection. In February 2009, the FTC issued a comprehensive report based on a two-day debt collection workshop, with findings, conclusions, and recommendations.[1] The 2009 report concluded that the "law needs to be changed to require that debt collectors have better information, making it more likely their attempts to collect are for the right amount and are directed to the right consumer."[2] Similarly, in 2010, the Commission issued a report addressing debt collection litigation, finding that complaints filed in court often do not contain sufficient information about the debt(s) to allow consumers in their answers to admit or deny the allegations and to assert affirmative defenses.[3]

In its 2009 report, the Commission also found that "[t]he most significant change in the debt collection business in recent years has been the advent and growth of debt buying."[4] Creditors often sell debt that they have not collected to "debt buyers." When debts are sold, the buyers receive information about the debtor and the debt from the sellers. Debt buyers also may resell the debt to other debt buyers. Many debts are purchased and resold several times over the course of years before either the debtor pays the debt or the debt's owner determines that the debt can be neither collected nor sold.

As the debt buyer industry has expanded, the Commission also has seen a significant rise in the number of debt collection complaints it received directly from consumers. Many consumers reported that the debt collectors who contacted them attempted to collect debts they did not owe or, if they did owe a debt, more than what was owed.[5]

Because of the important role that debt buying now plays and the possible link between debt buying and consumer protection problems, the Commission determined that a better understanding of the debt buying industry was critical to future policy and law enforcement work in this area. Thus, in December 2009, the

---

1   FEDERAL TRADE COMMISSION, COLLECTING CONSUMER DEBTS: THE CHALLENGES OF CHANGE –A WORKSHOP REPORT (2009) [hereinafter CHALLENGES OF CHANGE], *available at* http://www.ftc.gov/bcp/workshops/debtcollection/dcwr.pdf.

2   *Id.* at i.

3   FEDERAL TRADE COMMISSION, REPAIRING A BROKEN SYSTEM: PROTECTING CONSUMERS IN DEBT COLLECTION LITIGATION AND ARBITRATION (2010) [hereinafter REPAIRING A BROKEN SYSTEM], *available at* http://www.ftc.gov/os/2010/07/ debtcollectionreport.pdf. This report also found that during the collection process, consumers may unknowingly waive statute of limitations defenses that they could otherwise raise.

4   CHALLENGES OF CHANGE, *supra* note 1, at 13.

5   For example, in 2009, consumers filed 27,420 complaints that were coded in the Consumer Sentinel database as "falsely represents character, amount, or status of debt." These complaints represented 31.1% of all complaints about debt collectors. In addition, consumers filed 10,158 complaints that were coded in the Consumer Sentinel database as "refuses to verify the debt after debtor makes a written request." These complaints represented 11.5% of all complaints about debt collectors. Note that some consumers filed complaints reporting both of these types of practices. Note also that some complaints assigned to these codes do not report that collectors attempted to collect from the wrong person or the wrong amount.

Commission commenced an extensive and rigorous study of debt buying, including the sellers and buyers of debts as well as the types and amounts of debt sold. As part of the study, the Commission sought to obtain a better understanding of the process that debt owners use to sell debts to debt buyers, the terms and conditions of their purchase and sale agreements, and the information that debt buyers obtain and use in connection with acquiring and collecting on debts.

In this study, the Commission acquired and analyzed a massive amount of information relating to debt buying. Most significantly, the FTC used compulsory process to obtain extensive narratives and empirical data from nine large debt buyers. The Commission engaged in rigorous assessment of the information obtained, including a detailed empirical analysis. It also drew on its enforcement, research, and policy activities related to debt collection, and it reviewed the growing volume of professional literature concerning debt buying. The study focused on large debt buyers because they account for most of the debt purchased but did not address the practices of smaller debt buyers that, in the FTC's experience, are a frequent source of consumer protection concerns. As noted in various places in the report, it is important to consider this limitation when evaluating certain of the study's findings. Another limitation of the study is that the FTC did not directly assess the accuracy of the information that debt buyers used in collecting purchased debts or filing lawsuits on this debt.

The following report presents the results of the Commission's debt buyer study. Part II describes the legal framework for debt buying. Part III is a description of the study's methodology, and Part IV is a discussion of the genesis and current operation of the debt buying industry. Part V describes the debt buying process, including the creation and marketing of debt portfolios, bidding on such portfolios, the prices paid for various types of debt, and the purchase and sales agreements used in the sales. Part VI evaluates the information debt buyers have, or have access to, at critical junctures in collecting and suing to recover on debts, and the frequency with which debts are disputed and verified. Part VII discusses the collection of older debts. Finally, Part VIII is a brief conclusion.

II. LEGAL FRAMEWORK FOR DEBT BUYING

Federal and state laws apply to the conduct and information practices of debt buyers. In 1977, Congress passed the Fair Debt Collection Practices Act ("FDCPA")[6] to "eliminate abusive debt collection practices by debt collectors, to insure that those debt collectors who refrain from using [such] practices are not competitively disadvantaged," and to encourage states to take measures protecting consumers from abusive debt collection practices.[7] From 1977 until 2011, the Federal Trade Commission was the federal agency empowered to administer the FDCPA, as well as primarily responsible for enforcing it. In July 2011, pursuant to the Dodd-Frank Wall Street Reform and Consumer Protection Act of 2010 ("Dodd-Frank Act"),[8] Congress transferred to the Consumer Financial Protection Bureau ("CFPB") the FTC's role of administering the FDCPA.[9] Both the FTC and the CFPB enforce the FDCPA.

The FDCPA governs the activities of "debt collectors," a term that includes debt buyers. The Act defines "debt collector" as "any person who uses any instrumentality of interstate commerce or the mails in any business the principal purpose of which is the collection of any debts, or who regularly collects . . . debts owed or due . . . to another."[10] The FDCPA does not govern the debt collection activities of "creditors" collecting their own debts.[11] The term "creditor" is defined as "any person who offers or extends credit creating a debt or to whom a debt is owed, but [not] any person to the extent that he receives an assignment or transfer of a debt in default solely for the purpose of facilitating collection of such debt."[12] Some debt buyers have argued that because they collect debts they own, not debts others own, the FDCPA does not govern their activities because they are creditors. In the seminal decision in *Kimber v. Federal Financial Corp.*, the court rejected that argument, holding that debt buyers that seek to recover on debts that were in

---

6   15 U.S.C. §§ 1692-1692p (2006 & Supp. IV 2010).

7   FDCPA § 802(e), 15 U.S.C. § 1692(e) (2006).

8   Pub. L. No. 111-203, 124 Stat 1376 (2010).

9   Dodd-Frank Act §1089; FDCPA § 814, 15 U.S.C. § 1692*l*.

10   FDCPA § 803(6), 15 U.S.C. § 1692a(6).

11   *Id.* § 803(6)(A), 15 U.S.C. § 1692a(6)(A).

12   *Id.* § 803(4), 15 U.S.C. § 1692a(4).

default when the debt buyers acquired them are debt collectors for purposes of the FDCPA.[13] Since *Kimber*, many other courts have concluded that such debt buyers are debt collectors for purposes of the FDCPA.[14]

The FDCPA thus applies to the activities of debt buyers that purchase accounts in default. The FDCPA prohibits debt collectors from engaging in unfair, deceptive, and abusive acts and practices in collecting on debts.[15] The FDCPA also requires that debt collectors provide consumers, within five days after initially contacting them, with "validation notices" setting forth some basic information about their debts and their rights during the debt collection process.[16] Further, if consumers "dispute" a debt within thirty days of receipt of validation notices, then debt collectors must suspend collection efforts until they obtain "verification" of the debts.[17] Validation notices and the process of disputing and verifying debts are discussed in detail below in Part VI, Information in the Collection Process.

In addition to the FDCPA, debt buyers and other debt collectors are governed by Section 5 of the Federal Trade Commission Act, which prohibits "unfair or deceptive acts or practices in or affecting commerce."[18] An act or practice is "unfair" under Section 5 if it "causes or is likely to cause substantial injury to consumers which is not reasonably avoidable by consumers themselves and not outweighed by countervailing benefits to consumers or to competition."[19] A practice is considered "deceptive" if "there is a representation, omission or practice that is likely to mislead the consumer acting reasonably in the circumstances, to the consumer's detriment."[20] Certain practices by debt buyers and other collectors that

---

13   668 F. Supp. 1480 (M.D. Ala. 1987). The *Kimber* court explained that Congress excluded creditors from the FDCPA because they "generally are restrained by the desire to protect their good will when collecting past due accounts," while debt collectors "are likely to have no future contact with the consumer and often are unconcerned with the consumer's opinion of them." *Id.* at 1486 (quoting S. Rep. No. 95-382, *reprinted in* 1977 U.S.C.C.A.N. 1695, 1696). Debt buyers that purchase debts that are in default, unlike original creditors, are not constrained by the need to maintain good will when seeking to recover on the debts of consumers who have defaulted. Debt buyers thus "are simply independent collectors of past due debts and thus clearly fall within the group Congress intended the Act to cover." *Id.* at 1486.

14   *See, e.g., McKinney v. Cadleway Props., Inc.*, 548 F.3d 496, 501 (7th Cir. 2008) ("[T]he purchaser of a debt in default is a debt collector for purposes of the FDCPA even though it owns the debt and is collecting for itself."); *FTC v. Check Investors, Inc.*, 502 F.3d 159, 170-74 (3d Cir. 2007) ("[A]n assignee may be deemed a 'debt collector' if the obligation is already in default when it is assigned.") (quoting *Pollice v. Nat'l Tax Funding, L.P.*, 225 F.3d 379, 403-04 (3d Cir. 2000)); *Schlosser v. Fairbanks Capital Corp.*, 323 F.3d 534, 536 (7th Cir. 2003) ("[T]he Act treats assignees as debt collectors if the debt sought to be collected was in default when acquired by the assignee, and as creditors if it was not.").

15   FDCPA §§ 806-808, 15 U.S.C. §§ 1692d-f.

16   *Id.* § 809(a), 15 U.S.C. § 1692g(a).

17   *Id.* § 809(b), 15 U.S.C. § 1692g(b).

18   15 U.S.C. § 45(a)(1) (2006).

19   *Id.* § 45(n) (codifying the Commission's unfairness analysis); *see also* Letter from the FTC to Hon. Wendell Ford and Hon. John Danforth, Committee on Commerce, Science and Transportation, United States Senate, Commission Statement of Policy on the Scope of Consumer Unfairness Jurisdiction, *reprinted in In re Int'l Harvester Co.*, 104 F.T.C. 949, 1079, 1074 n.3 (1984) ("Unfairness Policy Statement").

20   Federal Trade Commission Policy Statement on Deception, *appended to In re Cliffdale Assocs., Inc.*, 103 F.T.C. 110, 174–83 (1984) ("Deception Policy Statement").

violate the FDCPA also violate Section 5 of the FTC Act.[21] The Commission uses the FTC Act to stop unfair or deceptive debt collection practices by creditors[22] and others that are not covered by the FDCPA.[23]

Another federal statute governing debt buyers is the Fair Credit Reporting Act ("FCRA"),[24] which imposes data privacy and accuracy standards on consumer reporting agencies (often referred to as "credit bureaus") and entities, including debt buyers and other debt collectors, that use consumer reports or furnish information to them. Debt collectors and other entities that furnish information to consumer reporting agencies (often referred to as "furnishers") violate the FCRA if they report information they know or have reasonable cause to believe is inaccurate.[25] The FCRA also allows consumers to dispute the completeness or accuracy of information, including delinquent accounts, on their credit reports, and requires furnishers to conduct "reasonable investigations" of disputes submitted directly to them concerning the accuracy of information reported.[26]

In addition to these federal statutes, many states have enacted laws, issued regulations, or adopted court rules that restrict or limit the activities of debt collectors or debt buyers. Many of the state laws are comparable to the FDCPA in prohibiting unfair, deceptive, or abusive debt collection practices.[27] Some also require that debt buyers be licensed to collect from consumers located in that state.[28] State regulations also may address collection activities in which some debt buyers engage, such as collecting on time-barred debt.[29]

---

21   In its enforcement actions against debt collectors covered by the FDCPA, the Commission often alleges that the same practices violate both Section 5 and one or more FDCPA provisions. *See, e.g.*, Complaint at ¶¶ 41-49, *United States v. Luebke Baker & Assocs.*, No. 1:12-cv-1145 (C.D. Ill. May 11, 2012), *available at* http://www.ftc.gov/opa/2012/05/luebkenr.shtm; Complaint at ¶¶ 35-50, *United States v. West Asset Mgmt., Inc.*, No. 1:11-cv-0746 (N.D. Ga. Mar. 10, 2011), *available at* http://www.ftc.gov/opa/2011/03/wam.shtm.

22   The Commission does not, however, have jurisdiction over banks, thrifts, and federal credit unions. 15 U.S.C. § 45.

23   *See, e.g.*, *FTC v. Payday Financial, LLC*, No. 11-3017 (D.S.C. Sept. 6, 2011), *available at* http://www.ftc.gov/opa/2011/09/payday.shtm; *FTC v. Cash Today, Ltd*, No. 3:08-CV-590 (D. Nev. Nov. 6, 2008), *available at* http://www.ftc.gov/opa/2008/11/cashtoday.shtm.

24   15 U.S.C. §§ 1681-1681x (2006 & Supp. IV 2010).

25   FCRA § 623(a)(1)(A), 15 U.S.C. § 1681s-2(a)(1)(A).

26   *Id.* § 611(a), 15 U.S.C. § 1681i(a); *id.* § 623(b)(1), 15 U.S.C. §1681s-2(b)(1); 16 C.F.R. § 660.4; 12 C.F.R § 1022.43. Unlike the thirty-day period for written disputes under FDCPA § 809(b), the FCRA regulations require furnishers to take the same steps no matter when a consumer submits a written dispute.

27   *See, e.g.*, Cal. Civ. Code §§ 1788-1788.33 (West 2012); 18 Pa. Cons. Stat. Ann. § 7311 (West 2012); Wash Rev. Code § 19.16.250 (2012); *Pub. Finance Co. v. Van Blaricome*, 324 N.W.2d 716, 724 (Iowa 1982) ("Congress passed a Fair Debt Collection Practices Act in 1977 which is similar to the Iowa act."); Lawrence A. Young and Jeffery D. Coulter, Practicing Law Inst., *Recent Developments in Fair Debt Collection Practices Act, State Collection Law and Debt Collection Class Action Litigation*, at 553, 592 (PLI Corporate Law and Practice, Course Handbook Ser. No. B7-7188, 1997) ("A state debt collection act may have many provisions that parallel those in the FDCPA.").

28   *See, e.g.*, Idaho Code Ann. § 26-2223 (2012); Mass. Gen. Laws Ann. ch. 93, § 24A (West 2012); N.C. Gen. Stat. Ann. § 58-70-1 (West 2012).

29   *See, e.g.*, 940 Mass. Code Regs. 7.00 (2012); N.M. Code R. § 12.2.12.9 (LexisNexis 2012); Tex. Fin. Code Ann. § 392 (West 2012).

States also are increasingly imposing more rigorous standards on the conduct of debt collectors (including debt buyers) in litigation to recover on debts.[30]

Finally, in addition to these legal requirements, industry self-regulation may govern the conduct of debt buyers that belong to trade associations. DBA International, the largest trade association of debt buyers, has issued standards of conduct of its members.[31] In early 2012, DBA International announced that it had created a Debt Buyer Certification Task Force to assess the feasibility of a comprehensive National Debt Buyer Certification Program, and the work of this task force is continuing.[32] ACA International, Inc., the largest trade association of debt collectors, also has issued standards of conduct for debt collectors, which would apply to the conduct of its members that are debt buyers.[33]

---

30 *See, e.g.*, Md. R. 3-306; 2009 N.C. Sess. Laws 573; Admin. Directive, No. 2011-1, *Consumer Debt Collection Actions* (Del. Ct. C.P. Mar. 16, 2011), *available at* http://www.courts.delaware.gov/CommonPleas/docs/AD2011-1ConsumerDebt0.pdf.

31 DBA Int'l, Ethics Rules and Ethical Considerations for DBA Members, *available at* http://www.dbainternational.org/what_is_dba/code_of_ethics.asp. DBA International represents more than 600 member organizations, including professional debt buyer companies as well as vendor and affiliate companies. DBA Int'l, Comments for the FTC Debt Collection Workshop 3 (June 2, 2007), *available at* http://www.ftc.gov/os/comments/debtcollectionworkshop/529233-00010.pdf; *DBA International Member Roster*, DBA Int'l, http://www.dbainternational.org/membership/roster.asp (last updated Nov. 30, 2012).

32 *DBA International Appoints Members of Certification Task Force*, DBA Int'l (Apr. 25, 2012), http://www.dbainternational.org/news/dba_taskforce2.asp; *DBA International to Launch Certification Task Force*, DBA Int'l (Feb. 17, 2012), http://www.dbainternational.org/news/dba_taskforce.asp.

33 ACA Int'l, Code of Ethics and Code of Operations 4 (rev. ed. 2010) [hereinafter ACA Code of Ethics], *available at* http://www.acainternational.org/files.aspx?p=/images/12909/codeofethics-ops_2010.pdf. The current ACA Code of Ethics was originally adopted on July 25, 2007. *Id.* ACA International represents more than 5,000 members, including third-party collection agencies, debt buyers, attorneys, creditors, and vendor affiliates. *About ACA*, ACA Int'l, http://www.acainternational.org/about.aspx (last visited Jan. 4, 2013). As of 2007, ACA represented approximately 95 percent of debt collectors located in the United States. Rozanne M. Andersen & Andrew M. Beato, ACA Int'l, Comments of ACA International Regarding the Debt Collection Workshop 7 n.6 (June 6, 2007), *available at* http://www.ftc.gov/comments/debtcollectionworkshop/529233-00016.pdf.

III. STUDY METHODOLOGY

The findings, conclusions, and recommendations set forth in this report are based on an analysis of data and information obtained from debt buyers, the FTC's extensive experience in debt collection matters, and a review of prior research, professional literature, and information elicited from industry representatives, consumer advocates, government officials, academics, and others.

A. DATA COLLECTED FROM DEBT BUYERS

In December 2009, the Commission issued identical orders to nine of the largest debt buyers in the United States.[34] The nine firms receiving orders were chosen from among the ten largest purchasers of consumer debt in 2008, as estimated by The Nilson Report.[35] According to this same report, debt buyers in 2008 purchased $72.3 billion in consumer debt, including credit card, medical, utility, auto, and mortgage debt. Of that total, $55.5 billion, or 76.8%, was credit card debt bought directly from issuers. The nine selected debt buyers collectively purchased 76.1% of all consumer debt sold in 2008. The nine debt buyers that received orders were:

- Sherman Financial Group, LLC

- Encore Capital Group Inc.

- eCAST Settlement Corp.

- NCO Portfolio Management, Inc.

- Arrow Financial Services, LLC

- Portfolio Recovery Associates, L.L.C.

- Unifund Corp.

- B-Line, LLC

- Asta Funding, Inc.

---

34 The FTC has the authority to issue such orders under Section 6(b) of the Federal Trade Commission Act, 15 U.S.C. § 46(b) (2006). Although there are hundreds, if not thousands, of debt buyers in the United States, the Commission limited its orders to nine debt buyers because seeking information from more than nine debt buyers would have triggered Paperwork Reduction Act requirements that would have significantly delayed the study. *See* 44 U.S.C. § 3502(3)(A)(i) (2006).

35 *Credit Card Debt Sales in 2008*, 921 Nilson Rep. 10 (Mar. 2009) [hereinafter Nilson Report]. See the source note to Table 1 in the Table Appendix regarding Nilson Report data. The nine debt buyers purchased $55.0 billion (76.1%) of the estimated total $72.3 billion in debt sold in 2008. One other large debt buyer, Asset Acceptance, was under FTC investigation at the time the FTC issued its orders. The Commission has since entered into a settlement agreement with Asset Acceptance. *See United States v. Asset Acceptance, LLC*, No. 8:12-cv-182 (M.D. Fla. Jan. 31, 2012), *available at* http://www.ftc.gov/opa/2012/01/asset.shtm. See *infra* notes 199-201 and accompanying text for further discussion of this case.

Credit card debt was by far the most common type of debt these debt buyers purchased. In 2008, these buyers purchased 78.2% of all credit card debt that card issuers sold directly to debt buyers.[36] **Table 1** shows the total amount of debt purchased and the amount of debt bought directly from credit card issuers in 2008 by each of the nine debt buyers.[37]

Although the study obtained information from debt buyers that collectively purchased most (76.1%) of the debt in the United States, it did not examine information from small debt buyers, debt buyers that purchase most of their debt from other debt buyers, and debt buyers under FTC investigation at the time the agency issued its 6(b) orders. The Commission's experience suggests that these types of debt buyers are likely to be a source of significant consumer protection problems.[38] Therefore, their practices may be an appropriate area for future study and examination.

The FTC's orders required that the recipients produce extensive data about their business practices and how they receive, acquire, and transfer information about consumer debts. Each debt buyer received an identical order, a model order of which is attached to this report as **Exhibit 1**. **Technical Appendix A** contains an overview of some of the key data requests. The data provided in response to these requests are described in detail throughout the body of the report and the appendices.

The debt buyers submitted data from more than 5,000 portfolios purchased during the three-year study period. These portfolios contained nearly 90 million consumer accounts, reflecting nearly $143 billion in consumer debt (face value). The nine firms spent nearly $6.5 billion to acquire these debts from both credit issuers and resellers of debt.[39]

Most of the empirical analysis conducted for this report is based on data submitted by six of the nine debt buyers. One of the debt buyers receiving the Commission's order, Arrow Financial Services, exited the debt buying business in the middle of the sampling period and did not have the infrastructure to provide all of the data necessary for the analysis. In addition, two other debt buyers receiving the Commission's

---

36 Nilson Report, *supra* note 35, at 10. The nine debt buyers purchased $43.4 billion (78.2%) of the $55.5 billion in credit card debt purchased directly from card issuers in 2008. *Id.*

37 Two of the debt buyers, eCAST Settlement Corp. and B-Line, LLC, purchase only debts of consumers who have filed bankruptcy. Some of the other seven debt buyers also purchase a percentage of bankruptcy accounts, but the majority of their purchases are debts of consumers who have not filed for bankruptcy protection at or prior to the time of the debt purchases.

38 For example, the Commission's action against Asset Acceptance included allegations that the company could not substantiate claims it made about debts and that it frequently sought to collect the wrong amount or from the wrong consumer. Complaint at ¶¶ 54-55, *United States v. Asset Acceptance, LLC*, No. 8:12-cv-182 (M.D. Fla. Jan. 30, 2012), *available at* http://www.ftc.gov/opa/2012/01/asset.shtm; *see also* Kaulkin Ginsberg's Global Debt Buying Report: Experts Analyze the Worldwide Debt Buying Market 32 (2006) [hereinafter Global Debt Buying] ("Buyers in the secondary market also need to be concerned about purchasing fraudulent accounts that are comprised of inaccurate or even fictitious data. . . . So while the secondary market for delinquent debts provides smaller debts buyers with opportunities to acquire portfolios that they would otherwise be unable to source from creditors, this process is not without its risks. These risks increase significantly with the number of times that a portfolio has been bought and sold.").

39 *See infra* **Table 2** and **Technical Appendix D**.

orders, B-Line, LLC and eCAST Settlement Corp., specialize in purchasing bankruptcy debt. Because of the particular practices of this specialized type of debt buyer, they also could not provide much of the data necessary for the analysis. As a result, these three firms were excluded from most of the empirical analysis.

B. OTHER SOURCES OF INFORMATION

In addition to information obtained from the selected debt buyers, the FTC considered research and professional literature related to debt buying, including articles and reports from academics,[40] news sources,[41] consulting firms,[42] and government entities.[43] The Commission also surveyed and reviewed publications from industry and consumer groups.[44]

FTC staff elicited additional information through meetings with consumer advocates and industry representatives. Staff met with attorneys from the National Consumer Law Center and several attorneys in private practice who frequently represent consumers in lawsuits alleging illegal collection practices. Staff also met with representatives from two industry organizations: DBA International, which has approximately 600 active debt buying members, and ACA International, whose Asset Buyers Division has approximately 350 members. The Commission further considered information obtained during the staff's meeting with

---

40   *See, e.g.*, Christopher R. Drahozal & Samantha Zyontz, *Creditor Claims in Arbitration and in Court*, 7 Hastings Bus. L.J. 77 (2011); Judith Fox, *Do We Have a Debt Collection Crisis? Some Cautionary Tales of Debt Collection in Indiana*, 24 Loy. Consumer L. Rev. 355 (2012); Timothy E. Goldsmith & Natalie Martin, *Testing Materiality Under the Unfair Practices Acts: What Information Matters When Collecting Time-Barred Debts?*, 64 Consumer Fin. L.Q. Rep. 372 (2010); Peter A. Holland, *The One Hundred Billion Dollar Problem in Small Claims Court: Robo-Signing and Lack of Proof of Debt Buyer Cases*, 6 J. Bus. & Tech. L. 259 (2011); Mary Spector, *Debts, Defaults and Details: Exploring the Impact of Debt Collection Litigation on Consumers and Courts*, 6 Va. L. & Bus. Rev. 257 (2011); Lauren Goldberg, Note, *Dealing in Debt: The High Stakes World of Debt Collection After FDCPA*, 79 S. Cal. L. Rev. 711 (2006).

41   *See, e.g.*, Chris Seeres, *Debt Buyers on the Rise: More Arrest Warrants, Phantom Debts, Real Anguish*, Star Trib. (Minneapolis-St. Paul), June 27, 2010, at A1; David Segal, *Debt Collectors Face a Hazard: Writer's Cramp*, N.Y. Times, Nov. 1, 2010, at A1; Jessica Silver-Greenberg, *Boom in Debt Buying Fuels Another Boom — in Lawsuits*, Wall St. J., Nov. 29, 2010, at A1, *available at* http://online.wsj.com/article/SB20001424052702304510704575562212919179410.html.

42   *See, e.g.*, Global Debt Buying, *supra* note 38, at 26-27; Robert J. Andrews, *Debt Collection Agencies in the US*, IBISWorld Indus. Rep. 56144, at 14 (2010).

43   *See, e.g.*, U.S. Gov't Accountability Office, Credit Cards: Fair Debt Collection Practices Act Could Better Reflect the Evolving Debt Collection Marketplace and Use of Technology (2009) [hereinafter GAO FDCPA Report], *available at* http://www.gao.gov/assets/300/295588.pdf.

44   *See, e.g.*, DBA Int'l, DBA International's Paper on the Collection of Past Statute Debts (2007), *available at* http://www.ftc.gov/os/comments/debtcollectionworkshop/529233-00033.pdf; DBA Int'l, The Debt Buying Industry: A White Paper (2012), *available at* http://media.idahostatesman.com/smedia/2012/01/22/08/29/128SRK.So.36. pdf; Ernst & Young, The Impact of Third-Party Debt Collection on the National and State Economies (2012), *available at* http://www.acainternational.org/files.aspxp=/images/21594/2011acaeconomicimpactreport.pdf (commissioned by ACA International); Robert J. Hobbs & Rick Jurgens, Nat'l Consumer Law Ctr., The Debt Machine: How the Collection Industry Hounds Consumers and Overwhelms the Courts (2010), *available at* http://www.nclc.org/ images/pdf/pr-reports/debt-machine.pdf; Robert J. Hobbs & Chi Chi Wu, Nat'l Consumer Law Ctr., Model Family Financial Protection Act (2012), *available at* http://www.nclc.org/images/pdf/debt_collection/model_family_financial_ protection_act.pdf; Rachel Terp & Lauren Bowne, Past Due: Why Debt Collection Practices and the Debt Buying Industry Need Reform Now (2011), *available at* http://www.defendyourdollars.org/pdf/Past_Due_Report_2011. pdf.

Kaulkin Ginsberg Co., a market research firm that studies and consults with debt buyers and other members of the debt collection industry. FTC staff also met with the staff of the Consumer Financial Protection Bureau concerning the debt buyer industry generally and the availability of information about the industry. Staff sought to meet and confer with banks and the American Bankers Association to discuss their debt sales practices, but they declined to meet.

Finally, in preparing this report, the Commission relied on its own extensive experience in debt collection matters. The FTC has brought more than 80 law enforcement actions over more than three decades alleging illegal debt collection practices, including actions against debt buyers.[45] The Commission also has a robust history of conducting research and policy work related to debt collection issues. For example, as noted above, the FTC in recent years has hosted a series of public workshops and roundtables about debt collection issues, which culminated in the Commission issuing two comprehensive reports on the debt collection industry.[46]

---

45   *See, e.g.*, Complaint, *United States v. Luebke Baker & Assocs.*, No. 1:12-cv-1145 (C.D. Ill. May 11, 2012), *available at* http:// www.ftc.gov/opa/2012/05/luebkenr.shtm; *United States v. Asset Acceptance, LLC*, No. 8:12-cv-182 (M.D. Fla. Jan. 31, 2012), *available at* http://www.ftc.gov/opa/2012/01/asset.shtm; Complaint, *United States v. West Asset Management*, No. 1:11-cv-0746 (N.D. Ga. March 10, 2011), *available at* http://www.ftc.gov/opa/2011/03/wam.shtm; Complaint, *United States v. Whitewing Fin. Group, Inc.*, No. H-06-2102 (S.D. Tex. June 22, 2006), *available at* http://www.ftc.gov/opa/2006/07/ whitewing.shtm; Complaint, *FTC v. Capital Acquisitions & Mgmt Corp.*, No. 04C778 (N.D. Ill. Dec. 2, 2004), *available at* http://www.ftc.gov/opa/2006/12/camco.shtm.

46   *See* CHALLENGES OF CHANGE, *supra* note 1; REPAIRING A BROKEN SYSTEM, *supra* note 3. The Commission also held a workshop on debt collection technologies in 2011. *See Debt Collection 2.0: Protecting Consumers as Technologies Change*, FEDERAL TRADE COMMISSION (Apr. 28, 2011), http://www.ftc.gov/bcp/workshops/debtcollectiontech/index.shtml.

IV. THE DEBT BUYING MARKET

A. CONSUMER CREDIT AND DEBT BUYING

In a credit transaction, a creditor and a consumer enter into a contract under which the consumer receives money to make purchases now in exchange for promising to repay the creditor over time the amount received plus interest. Like other contracts, credit contracts are of little value if the parties cannot enforce them.[47] Creditors use debt collection to recover on these contracts if consumers do not repay the amounts they owe. Debt collection reduces the amounts that creditors lose from debts, both directly (by collecting on the debts) and indirectly (by making it more likely that consumers will incur debt only if they can and will repay it). By reducing the losses that creditors incur in providing credit, debt collection also allows creditors to provide more credit at lower prices – that is, at lower interest rates.[48]

Creditors use a variety of methods to recover on debts they own. Creditors can and often do collect on their own debts. In addition, many creditors retain others to collect debts on their behalf. Creditors retain such "third-party" debt collectors for many reasons. Third-party debt collectors often have greater expertise (*e.g.*, knowledge of the legal requirements to collect debt in a particular jurisdiction) or enhanced infrastructure (*e.g.*, a specialized database and communication technologies) that allow them to collect more efficiently than creditors can. The costs of acquiring such expertise or infrastructure may be impractical or inefficient for small creditors, but even large creditors may find third-party debt collection to be cost-efficient.

Although creditors traditionally either collected their debts themselves or retained a third-party debt collector to collect on their behalf, creditors now have a third option. Creditors may sell debts they own to debt buyers. Debt buyers, in turn, may either try to collect on purchased debts themselves, hire a third-party debt collector to recover on these debts for them, or resell these debts to other debt buyers. As with the collection of debts, the selling of debts by creditors decreases the losses they incur in extending credit, which, in turn, is likely to lead to an increase in the amount of credit extended and a decrease in the price of that credit.[49]

---

47   Benjamin E. Hermalin, Avery W. Katz, & Richard Craswell, *Contract Law, in* 1 HANDBOOK OF LAW AND ECONOMICS 99 (A. Mitchell Polinsky & Steven Shavell eds., 2007).

48   A number of empirical studies in the economics and finance literatures have found that greater efficiency in the judicial enforcement of credit contracts results in the greater availability or lower cost of credit. *See, e.g.,* MARCELA CRISTINI, RAMIRO MOYA, & ANDREW POWELL, INTER-AMERICAN DEV. BANK RESEARCH NETWORK WORKING PAPERS, THE IMPORTANCE OF AN EFFECTIVE LEGAL SYSTEM FOR CREDIT MARKETS: THE CASE OF ARGENTINA n.R-428 (2001); Kee-Hong Bae & Vidhan K. Goyal, *Creditor Rights, Enforcement, and Bank Loans,* 64 J. FIN. 823 n.2 (2009); Daniela Fabbri & Mario Padula, *Does Poor Legal Enforcement Make Households Credit-Constrained?* 28 J. BANKING & FIN. 2369 (2004); Tullio Jappelli, Marco Pagano, & Magda Bianco, *Courts and Banks: Effects of Judicial Enforcement on Credit Markets,* 37 J. MONEY, CREDIT, & BANKING 223 n.2 (2005); Luc Laeven & Giovanni Majnoni, *Does Judicial Efficiency Lower the Cost of Credit?* 29 J. BANKING & FIN. 1791 (2005).

49   *See supra* note 48.

In some circumstances, creditors may prefer to use third parties to collect debts rather than selling them to debt buyers. Third-party debt collection affords creditors greater control over how debt collectors interact with consumers, which may be important to creditors that are particularly interested in avoiding reputational harm (*e.g.*, hospitals collecting on medical debts). Ongoing cooperation between creditors and third-party debt collectors also may result in an efficient and effective collection process that leads to greater returns for creditors than selling the debts.

In other circumstances, creditors may prefer to sell their debts. For example, creditors may sell debts to avoid the costs of coordinating and monitoring the conduct of third-party debt collectors. Or creditors may choose to receive an immediate and guaranteed amount from debt sales rather than receiving a delayed and uncertain amount as a result of the efforts of third-party debt collectors.[50] Creditors also may use third-party collectors to try to recover on debts before selling them to debt buyers. Published studies and trade press accounts indicate that banks and other original creditors that sell charged-off debt often use third-party collectors to try to recover on the debt for a period of time before selling it.[51]

B. THE DEBT BUYING INDUSTRY

1. DEBT SELLERS AND DEBTS SOLD

The practice of creditors selling consumer debts on a large scale has its origins in the savings and loan crisis of the late 1980s and early 1990s.[52] During the crisis, the Resolution Trust Corporation, the federal entity assigned to liquidate failed thrifts, auctioned off nearly $500 billion in unpaid loans that creditors had owned.[53] The success of these sales in producing revenue persuaded other creditors to commence selling their debts.[54]

According to industry sources, two broad trends during the first decade of the twenty-first century fostered the growth of the debt buying industry.[55] First, consumers took on increasing amounts of revolving

---

50 *See* Andersen & Beato, *supra* note 33, at 29.

51 *Bad-Debt Prices Up Amid Supply Shortage*, COLLECTIONS & CREDIT RISK (July 2, 2010), http://www.collectionscreditrisk. com/news/bad-debt-prices-up-amid-supply-shortage-3002377-1.html ("[D]ebt prices dropped in 2009 as the quality of the debt coming into the market declined because of the severity of the recession. This led many lenders to work charge-off debt longer in hopes of earning a better return than they could by selling it."); Robert Hunt, *Collecting Consumer Debt in America*, FED. RESERVE BANK OF PHILA. BUS. REV., Q2 2007, at 12 ("In the case of credit cards, for example, creditors typically hire third-party collectors at 180 days, the point at which the creditor charges off the balance."). Additionally, publicly-traded Encore Capital Group has stated in its 10-K report for the fiscal year ending December 31, 2008, at page 10, "we believe that issuers of credit cards are increasingly using outsourced, off-shore alternatives in connection with their collection of delinquent accounts in an effort to reduce costs. If these off-shore efforts are successful, these issuers may decrease the number of portfolios they offer for sale and increase the purchase price for portfolios they offer for sale."

52 Andrews, *supra* note 42, at 14; Goldberg, *supra* note 40, at 725; Seeres, *supra* note 41, at 1A.

53 Andrews, *supra* note 42, at 14; Seeres, *supra* note 41, at 1A; Silver-Greenberg, *supra* note 41.

54 Andrews, *supra* note 42, at 14.

55 GLOBAL DEBT BUYING, *supra* note 38, at 5.

debt, especially credit card debt, as well as other non-revolving personal debts, such as student loans, which meant that creditors generally had more debt available for collection or sale. Second, most major credit card issuers (most of which are large banks) changed their overall accounts receivable management strategies to incorporate the routine sale of debts to others.[56]

Today, the market for the sale of debt has evolved such that many creditors appear to be able to quickly monetize delinquent debts. Perhaps the most important source of debts for the debt buyer market is so-called "charged-off debt."[57] After the passage of time, banks must "charge off" credit card debts to comply with federal banking regulations.[58] In contrast, cash proceeds from the sale of debt (including credit card debt) can be counted as assets for capital requirements. In a 2009 study of credit card debt collection, the Government Accountability Office found that five of the six largest credit card issuers sold at least some of their delinquent credit card debt to debt buyers.[59]

Industry-wide data show that bank sales of credit card debt directly to debt buyers account for 75% or more of all debt sold.[60] Even though the total amount of debt that buyers purchase has varied substantially over time, credit card debt has consistently comprised about 75% of the debt sold to debt buyers.[61]

---

56   *Id.* at 5, 19.

57   Creditors consider consumers who are late in paying as being "delinquent" on their debts. Creditors may continue to collect on delinquent debts, but after a period of time creditors consider consumers to be in "default" on their debts. Creditors may continue to collect on debts in default, but after the passage of a specified period of time, creditors must "charge-off" such debts, that is, no longer treat them as assets for capital requirements under federal banking regulations.

58   Federal regulations prohibit banks and other depository institutions from counting toward their capital requirements debts that are in bankruptcy or delinquent more than a specified number of days. Banks and other depository institutions specifically must charge off installment loan debts by the end of the month in which the debts become 120 days past due, credit card loan debts by the end of the month in which they become 180 days past due, and debts in in bankruptcy within 60 days of the bank's receipt of notification that consumers have filed for bankruptcy. Uniform Retail Credit Classification and Account Management Policy, 65 Fed. Reg. 36903-01 (June 12, 2000). Although banks and other depository institutions cannot count charged-off debts toward their capital requirements, these debts remain their assets and they can continue to seek a return on these assets through collecting on them or selling them to debt buyers. Note that different regulatory and accounting rules may be applicable to the delinquent debts of creditors that are not depository institutions (*e.g.*, auto lenders, telecommunications companies, utility providers, hospitals, etc.).

59   GAO FDCPA REPORT, *supra* note 43, at 26. The GAO's methodology for its study included interviewing representatives of the six largest credit card issuers (as measured by total outstanding credit card loans, as of December 31, 2007).

60   *See infra* **Table 3**. Credit card debts are also asserted to be the largest source of business for the third-party debt collectors that owners of debts – often banks – hire to collect. *See* Andrews, *supra* note 42, at 16.

61   ACA International reported that debt buyers purchased $110 billion, face value, in debts in 2005, and that 90 percent of these, or $99 billion in face value, were credit card debts. *See* Andersen & Beato, *supra* note 33, at 40. These amounts are well in excess of the amounts reported by *The Nilson Report*. NILSON REPORT, *supra* note 35. The difference may be due to the inclusion of debt sales from one debt buyer to another in the ACA International figures; it is also possible that ACA International and *The Nilson Report* use different methods of estimating credit card and total debt sales, and therefore arrive at different estimates.

In the Commission's study, 62% of portfolios purchased by the debt buyers were credit card portfolios.[62] Credit card debt also accounted for 71% of the total amount spent by the debt buyers to purchase debts and comprised 65% of the face value of all debts acquired.[63]

2. DEBT BUYERS

Since the commencement of large-scale sales of debts in the late 1980s, the number and variety of debt buyers in the marketplace have evolved.[64] Two large debt buyers, Commercial Financial Systems, Inc. and Creditrust Corporation, entered the debt buying market in a substantial manner in the late 1980s, but both firms had filed for bankruptcy by the end of the 1990s.[65] In the early 2000s, a number of smaller debt buyers entered the market to fill the gap that their departure created.[66] The number and type of debt buyers expanded rapidly in the 2000s, especially during the period from 2004-06,[67] as a result of, among other things, increases in the amount of debt available for purchase and the ready availability of capital to finance debt-buying enterprises and debt purchases.[68] This expansion slowed during the latter part of the last decade because of decreases in the amount of debt available for sale, the inability of consumers to repay their debts as a result of the economic downturn, and the unavailability of capital.[69]

Even though expansion abated somewhat in recent years, there now appear to be hundreds, if not thousands, of entities of varying sizes that purchase debts.[70] While there are many debt buyers, large debt buyers purchase most debt. In particular, as discussed above, the nine debt buyers the Commission studied purchased 76.1% of all consumer debt sold in 2008.[71]

In general, there do not appear to be significant barriers to entry into the debt buying industry. While some states require that debt buyers be licensed as debt collectors, state licensing requirements do not appear

---

62 *See infra* **Table 4** and **Technical Appendix D**. This percentage excludes portfolios that were identified by debt buyers as bankruptcy portfolios. As discussed in Technical Appendix D, however, we estimated that at least 60% of all bankruptcy portfolios were comprised of credit card debt.

63 *Id.* These percentages exclude portfolios that were identified by debt buyers as bankruptcy portfolios.

64 *See generally* TERP & BOWNE, *supra* note 44, at 2-4.

65 GLOBAL DEBT BUYING, *supra* note 38, at 5.

66 *Id.*

67 Darren Waggoner, *Debt-Buying Leaders Consider 2010 Outlook*, COLLECTIONS & CREDIT RISK (Jan. 5, 2009), http://www.collectionscreditrisk.com/news/debt-buying-leaders-consider-2010-outlook-3000124-1.html.

68 NILSON REPORT, *supra* note 35, at 10; *Debt-Buying Leaders Consider 2010 Outlook*, CARDLINE, Jan. 8, 2010.

69 *Bad-Debt Market Prices Up, Supply Down*, COLLECTIONS & CREDIT RISK, May 23, 2011; *Investors Return to Debt Buying: Prices Still High*, COLLECTIONS & CREDIT RISK, July 2010, at 21.

70 *See* DBA Int'l, Comments for the FTC Debt Collection Workshop, *supra* note 31, at 2 ("[T]here are hundreds (if not thousands) of entities purchasing debt . . . ."); Silver-Greenberg, *supra* note 41 ("More than 450 debt buyers scooped up an estimated $100 billion in distressed loans [in 2009], according to the latest estimates by Kaulkin-Ginsberg, a debt collection industry advisor.").

71 *See* Robert M. Hunt, Fed. Reserve Bank of Phila., Overview of the Collections Industry, Presentation at the 2007 FTC Debt Collection Workshop (Oct. 10, 2007), at 11 ("[The debt buying] market is relatively concentrated – 10 firms bought 81% of bad credit card debt in 2006.").

to impose any significant burdens on a new entrant, especially a new entrant that is already licensed in a state as a third-party debt collector.[72] Many of the thousands of third-party debt collectors could be considered potential entrants into the debt buying market because they have the expertise needed to collect on debt accounts.[73] Entry also could come from firms that have not previously been organized as third-party debt collectors. However, some industry analysts have noted that the ability of firms to purchase debt, especially credit card debt, may be contingent on the availability of financing in capital markets.[74]

Publicly traded debt buying firms consistently describe the debt buying market as being competitive and fragmented.[75] Vigorous competition among debt purchasers also appears to be indicated by the frequent changes in the rankings of the industry's largest firms. **Table 5** lists the 14 firms that have been ranked among the top purchasers of credit card debt between 2005 and 2011.[76] Four of these 14 firms are

---

72   *See, e.g.*, ALASKA STAT. § 08.24.110 (2012) (requiring an application, available at http://www.dced.state.ak.us/occ/pub/coa4106.pdf, fees, surety bond, and fingerprints; licensee must be at least nineteen years of age, possess a high-school equivalent education, and not been disbarred or convicted of a felony, larceny or embezzlement); NEV. REV. STAT. ANN. § 649.085 (LexisNexis 2011) (requiring an application, available at http://www.fid.state.nv.us/Applications/InstallmentLoan/Non-Depository_Initial_App.pdf, fees, surety bond, fingerprints, and financial statement; licensee must be a US citizen who will maintain an office in the US, and not been convicted of a felony or fraud or within ten years had a collection agency license suspended or revoked); TENN. CODE ANN. § 62-20-107 (2012) (requiring an application, available at http://www.tn.gov/commerce/boards/collect/documents/CSBCollectionAgencyapplication110911.pdf, fees, surety bond, and proposed six-month budget; licensee must not have within the last seven years been disbarred, convicted of fraud or a felony, or filed for bankruptcy).

73   *See* GLOBAL DEBT BUYING, *supra* note 38, at 122 ("Some debt buyers . . . expect increased competition from contingency collection agencies and collection law firms in the years to come. These companies, of course, already specialize in the collection of delinquent debt, and thereby have some of the resources necessary for success in the debt buying field."); Stephanie Eidelman, *Creditors Play an Unrecognized and Powerful Role in the Debt Collection Process*, FORBES (Nov. 29, 2011), http://www.forbes.com/sites/insidearm/2011/11/29/creditors-play-an-unrecognized-and-powerful-role-in-the-debt-collection-process/ ("There are approximately 5,000 third party debt collection agencies in the U.S. The majority of those are small companies with revenues under $1-2 million."). The Consumer Financial Protection Bureau has estimated that there are approximately 4,500 debt collection firms in the U.S. The CFPB further estimates that the median for annual receipts among collection firms is roughly $500,000. Defining Larger Participants in Certain Consumer Financial Product and Service Markets, 77 Fed. Reg. 9592, 9599 (proposed Feb. 17, 2012) (to be codified at 12 C.F.R. pt. 1090). Approximately 175 debt collection firms with annual receipts in excess of $10 million generate approximately 63 percent of collection receipts in the industry. Defining Larger Participants in Certain Consumer Financial Product and Service Markets, 77 Fed. Reg. at 9599; CONSUMER FIN. PROT. BUREAU. ANNUAL REPORT TO CONGRESS ON THE FAIR DEBT COLLECTION PRACTICES ACT 13 (2012), *available at* http://files.consumerfinance.gov/f/201203_cfpb_FDCPA_annual_report.pdf.

74   *See, e.g.*, GLOBAL DEBT BUYING, *supra* note 38, at 9 ("Debt buyers must be well capitalized to participate in [the credit card sector] of the [debt buying] market."); Mark Russell, *Credit Card Debt Buying Market Showing Signs of Life*, INSIDE ARM, July 20, 2011 ("Financing remains a challenge, particularly for newly formed debt buyers and small or mid-sized debt purchasing companies.").

75   *See, e.g.*, Asset Acceptance Capital Corp., Annual Report (Form 10-K), at 9 (Mar. 12, 2010); Asta Funding, Inc., Annual Report (Form 10-K), at 10 (Dec. 29, 2009); Encore Capital Group, Annual Report (Form 10-K), at 4 (Feb. 11, 2009); Portfolio Recovery Assocs., Inc, Annual Report (Form 10-K), at 12 (Feb. 16, 2010). NCO Group, the parent company of debt buyer NCO Portfolio Management, discussed competition in the broader category of business process outsourcing in its 10-K report for the year ended December 31, 2009, but also indicated, at p. 4, that the market for purchased debt portfolios was very competitive. *See* NCO Group, Inc., Annual Report (Form 10-K), at 4 (March 31, 2010).

76   This table is based upon various issues of the Nilson Report. *See, e.g.*, NILSON REPORT, *supra* note 35.

publicly-traded, and the rest are privately held.[77] As shown in the table, there is often substantial year-to-year variation in these rankings. Although Sherman Financial has been the largest purchaser of debts directly from credit issuers in all but one of the years presented, there have been some large swings in the firms claiming the second highest rank in purchases.[78] For example, NCO Portfolio Management held the second highest rank in 2005, but then dropped out of the top ten rankings for 2006 through 2008, edging back into the top 10 (in the ninth highest ranking) in 2009, but was not among the top 10 purchasers in 2010 or 2011.[79] In addition to the competition these debt buyers face from one another, they also may face potential competition from credit issuers, which may choose not to sell their debts and instead continue to collect the debts themselves or through contractual relationships with third-party debt collectors.[80]

---

77   The publicly-traded firms that were among the top 10 purchasers of debt directly from credit card issuers were Asset Acceptance Capital Corp., Asta Funding Inc., Encore Capital Group Inc., and Portfolio Recovery Associates. A fifth publicly-traded firm, First City Financial Corp., was not in the top 10 rankings.

78   Arrow Financial rose from the tenth highest ranking in 2005 to the second highest ranking in 2008, only to exit the industry thereafter. Encore Capital was ranked tenth among direct buyers from credit card issuers in 2006, but was ranked second in 2009, first in 2010, and then again second in 2011.

79   NCO Portfolio Management made a strategic business decision to reduce its participation in this segment of the market in 2009 and 2010. *See* NCO GROUP, INC., *supra* note 75, at 4.

80   *See, e.g.*, Asset Acceptance Capital Corp., *supra* note 75, at 9 ("We compete with a wide range of other purchasers of charged-off consumer receivables, third party collection agencies, other financial service companies and credit originators that manage their own consumer receivables."); Asta Funding, Inc., *supra* note 75, at 10 ("We compete with: other purchasers of consumer receivables, including third-party collection companies; and other financial services companies who purchase consumer receivables."); Encore Capital Group, *supra* note 75, at 4 ("We compete with a wide range of collection companies, financial services companies and a number of well-funded, entrants with limited experience in our industry. We also compete with traditional contingency collection agencies and in-house recovery departments."); Portfolio Recovery Associates, Inc., *supra* note 75, at 12 ("We face competition … [from] … other purchasers of defaulted consumer receivables portfolios, third-party contingent fee collection agencies and debt owners that manage their own defaulted consumer receivables rather than outsourcing them.").

V. THE DEBT BUYING PROCESS

Owners of debt create, market, offer, and sell portfolios of debt. Debt buyers identify, bid for, and purchase these portfolios. Purchase and sale agreements set forth the terms under which owners of debt sell debt portfolios to debt buyers. Among other things, these contracts state the information that owners of debt provide to debt buyers at the time of sale, as well as the information that debt buyers may obtain from them and on what terms after the time of sale. The interaction between potential sellers and buyers of debt in the debt buying process and the contracts between sellers and buyers are critical to understanding the use of information in the debt buying system.[81]

A. SELLER CREATION OF DEBT PORTFOLIOS

1. CREATION OF PORTFOLIOS BY ORIGINAL CREDITORS

Most original creditors try to collect on debts before selling them to others, whether by collecting on the debts themselves, hiring one or more third-party debt collectors, or both. Throughout the collection process, original creditors may decide to sell some or all of the debts they own and that they or their third-party debt collectors have not been able to recover.[82]

Debts sold by original creditors are typically bundled into portfolios.[83] Debts within original creditor portfolios generally share common attributes, such as the type of credit issued,[84] the elapsed time since the consumer accounts went into default, and the number of third-party debt collection firms with which creditors placed the accounts prior to the creditors offering them for sale. Other debt sellers may create portfolios with debts where the debtors share common features. For instance, some portfolios contain only debts from debtors with recent credit scores within a given range, or debtors whose last known address was within particular states. Debts that have been settled, challenged by consumers, or in active litigation are

---

81   Much of the discussion in Part V of this report is derived from confidential commercial information that debt buyers provided to the Commission about their company's business practices. To protect the debt buyers that submitted this information from harm to their ability to compete, the statements about business practices in this Part are not attributed to specific firms.

82   For example, an original creditor that first attempts to collect accounts internally, then places the accounts with one collection agency — the "primary" collection agency — then places the remaining accounts with a secondary collection agency, may sell a portion of the charged-off accounts at each collection stage (e.g., 25% immediately after charge-off, 25% after the primary agency, and 100% of remaining eligible accounts after the secondary agency; other creditors may refer the accounts to additional contingency collectors).

83   Bundling accounts into portfolios reduces the transactions costs of exchange.

84   Most debt sellers create portfolios with debts that are all the same type of debt. For example, banks may bundle credit card debts together into portfolios, but would not bundle together credit and medical debts, because banks do not typically extend medical credit. Similarly, issuers of medical credit would sell portfolios that were formed exclusively of medical debts, and not of telecommunications or auto loan debts. Some banks may bundle into a portfolio a variety of bank-issued or serviced credit products, such as nationally-branded credit cards ("Visa" or "Mastercard"), "private label" credit cards, credit card accounts issued by another bank acquired through merger, consumer loans, and overdrafts.

typically not included in portfolios. Under most purchase and sale agreements, a buyer can return these so-called "ineligible accounts" to the seller for a refund.[85]

When offering portfolios, sellers in the debt buying industry generally categorize the age of debt as follows:[86]

♦ **Fresh debts** are typically up to 6 months in age, and the original creditors sell them without making any attempt to collect following charge-off;

♦ **Primary debts** are typically up to 12 months in age, and the original creditors have hired one third-party debt collector to try to recover following charge-off; and

♦ **Secondary and tertiary debts** are typically up to 18 or 30 months in age respectively, and the original creditors have hired two or more third-party debt collectors to attempt to recover following charge-off.

Original creditors also sometimes create portfolios of debts of consumers who have filed for bankruptcy. Some debt buyers specialize in purchasing bankruptcy portfolios. Such portfolios are generally selected based on the type of bankruptcy protection sought, which is typically Chapter 7 or Chapter 13. In Chapter 7 bankruptcies, an individual's debts that are not satisfied by a sale of the debtor's non-exempt assets are discharged — that is, the consumer is no longer liable for them as a matter of law. In contrast, in Chapter 13 bankruptcy, an individual remains liable for all or part of debts as part of a repayment plan.[87] As shown in **Table 4**, debt buyers appear willing to pay more for debts for consumers in Chapter 13 compared to Chapter 7.[88]

Like non-bankruptcy portfolios, bankruptcy portfolios will typically be organized around a single type of debt, *e.g.*, credit card debts. Unlike non-bankruptcy portfolios, however, the debts within a given bankruptcy portfolio may not be categorized as "fresh," "primary," "secondary," or "tertiary," as those terms are used to describe debts not in bankruptcy.[89] Rather, portfolios of accounts in bankruptcy tend to be

---

85   *See infra* **Technical Appendix C**, at p. C-15 (discussing put-back rights).

86   *See, e.g.*, GLOBAL DEBT BUYING, *supra* note 38, at 26-27. Note that these terms and these time periods do not necessarily have a precise meaning within the industry.

87   In Chapter 7 bankruptcy, debt is generally discharged and the debtor is released from liability for the discharged debt. 11 U.S.C. § 727 (2006). The bankruptcy trustee sells the debtor's non-exempt assets and uses the proceeds to reimburse creditors. 11 U.S.C. §§ 704, 726 (2006 & Supp. IV 2010); *see also Liquidation Under the Bankruptcy Code*, ADMIN. OFF. U.S. CTS., http://www.uscourts.gov/FederalCourts/Bankruptcy/BankruptcyBasics/Chapter7.aspx (last visited Jan. 4, 2013). In Chapter 13 bankruptcy, an individual's debts are reorganized, and a repayment plan is developed whereby the debtor repays all or part of the debts owed. 11 U.S.C. §§ 1301-1330; *see also Individual Debt Adjustment*, ADMIN. OFF. U.S. CTS, http://www.uscourts.gov/FederalCourts/Bankruptcy/BankruptcyBasics/Chapter13.aspx (last visited Jan. 4, 2013).

88   *See also* GLOBAL DEBT BUYING, *supra* note 38, at 50 (describing varying prices for bankruptcy portfolios depending on the type of bankruptcy).

89   According to one of the debt buyers in the study, original creditors typically do not use the number of prior third-party collectors in developing criteria for inclusion in bankruptcy portfolios.

organized around the age of the debts based on the elapsed time since the consumer filed for bankruptcy, because the time of this event is more likely to predict when the bankruptcy proceedings will be resolved.[90]

2. CREATION OF PORTFOLIOS BY DEBT BUYERS AS RESELLERS

If the purchase and sale agreements under which debt buyers acquired debt do not limit their ability to resell debts in portfolios, some debt buyers may include these debts in portfolios they offer for sale to other debt buyers — that is, they become resellers that are sometimes called "secondary debt sellers." The debt buyers that purchase debts from resellers of debt are correspondingly sometimes known as "secondary debt buyers."

Resellers generally use one of three methods to create and develop portfolios to offer to debt buyers:

♦ Resellers may buy portfolios from an original creditor and then immediately sell the entire portfolio, as is, to debt buyers.

♦ Resellers may buy portfolios from an original creditor, repackage the debts into new portfolios based on more specific criteria, and then sell these portfolios to debt buyers. For example, a reseller may purchase a national portfolio of credit card debts, create state-specific portfolios from the national portfolio, and then resell the state-specific portfolios separately to other debt buyers.

♦ Resellers may buy portfolios from an original creditor, attempt to collect on the debts in the portfolio, and then sell some or all of the debts that it cannot collect to other debt buyers.[91]

Resellers apparently often create portfolios of debt at the specific request of another debt buyer. A debt buyer may contact a prospective reseller and identify the type or types of debts it seeks to purchase. The criteria that prospective purchasers use to identify debts for a resold portfolio might include some combination of the type of debts, the value of the debts, the age of the debts, the state in which the consumers reside, and the status of the debts (*e.g.*, debts in bankruptcy or debts of deceased consumers). In creating a portfolio that conforms to the potential purchaser's specifications, resellers generally include debts from a number of portfolios they own.

Some of the debt buyers from which the Commission received data in response to its 6(b) orders were resellers of debts. Most of the portfolios these firms created and sold to others contained only credit card debts. Some of them included a combination of two or more types of debts — for example, a combination of credit card debt and automobile loans. Other portfolios contained only automobile loans, personal loans, telecommunication debts, retail debts, or healthcare debts.

---

90   Indeed, some individual debts may be current at the time the consumer files for bankruptcy, because consumers generally file for bankruptcy based on their aggregate debt level relative to their assets and income.

91   *See* GLOBAL DEBT BUYING, *supra* note 38, at 29.

B. SELLER MARKETING OF PORTFOLIOS

After creating portfolios for sale, original creditors and resellers (collectively "sellers") market them to debt buyers. Sellers may directly contact buyers they think are well-qualified and try to persuade them to purchase portfolios. Debt buyer industry representatives report that some large sellers (*e.g.*, major credit card issuers) sell debts only to purchasers with well-established reputations and demonstrated financial strength. Large sellers apparently employ these selection criteria to decrease their risk of reputational harm as a result of the conduct of the debt buyers in collecting on debts as well as to decrease the sellers' credit risk. Some sellers use preexisting business relationships or specific contractual agreements to limit the buyers to which they sell their portfolios.

Other sellers of debt, however, market their portfolios much more broadly. Some sellers use mailing lists, clearinghouses, and telephone calls to inform potential buyers of portfolios they have for sale. Many sellers advertise on web sites the portfolios on which they are seeking bids from prospective buyers, or they use emails to alert potential buyers to purchase opportunities.

In addition to responding to seller-initiated marketing efforts, some debt buyers actively seek opportunities to purchase portfolios. Some debt buyers have in-house personnel who regularly contact sellers to see whether they are offering any portfolios for sale. Buyers also network, attend industry events, exhibit at trade shows, advertise in trade publications, maintain websites, and make contacts through industry associations, or other informal groups to contact sellers.

Once debt buyers learn that a seller is offering a particular portfolio, the buyers must determine whether to bid on the portfolio, and, if so, at what price. Sellers provide documents and information – known as "bid files" – to potential purchasers so that they can make such bidding decisions. The information that debt sellers include in bid files varies greatly by seller, portfolio type, and other factors. One debt buyer in the Commission's study, for example, indicated that debt brokers arranging sales on behalf of sellers[92] generally provide a "comprehensive" package to prospective purchasers, while the amount of information sellers provide in non-brokered sales is highly variable.

Although the information that debt sellers make available to prospective purchasers varies significantly, the most common part of bid files are "data files." Data files, usually one or more spreadsheets, provide information about individual debts in a portfolio (either a sample of the debts or all of them) such as consumers' names, addresses, phone numbers, and social security numbers; original account numbers; original balances; charge-off balances; charge-off dates; interest rates; the identity of original creditors;

---

92   A debt broker is someone who acts as an intermediary on behalf of the originator or reseller of debt. First-time debt buyers often purchase through brokers until they have built relationships sufficient to purchase debt directly. *See* ACA INT'L, BUYING RECEIVABLES 14 (3d ed. 2007).

date the account was opened; and last payment date.[93] Some information in the initial data file (usually information relating to the identity of debtors) may be redacted or "masked."

In addition to data files, sellers sometimes include "seller surveys" in bid files. Seller surveys are brief questionnaires that sellers prepare and complete to provide prospective purchasers with information such as the type of debt, original issuer, past collection or settlement efforts, portfolio selection criteria, and terms for obtaining documentation from the seller in the future. Some debt buyers stated that seller surveys usually are included in bid files. Such surveys, however, did not appear in some of the bid files that the Commission reviewed.[94]

Sellers occasionally include information in bid files other than data files and seller surveys. Some sellers may include a draft purchase and sale agreement with their preferred terms of sale and ask potential buyers to submit proposed changes to that agreement. Others may include additional documentation for specialized portfolios. Sellers of bankruptcy portfolios, for example, may provide the bankruptcy case number, chapter of the Bankruptcy Code, filing date, outstanding balance as of filing date, and proof of claim balance for the debts in portfolios.

C. BUYER ANALYSIS OF SELLER PORTFOLIO INFORMATION

Once they have received marketing and bid file information from sellers, potential purchasers analyze this information to determine whether, and for what price, they are willing to bid on the portfolio. Potential purchasers may use several methods of quantitative analysis to evaluate how much to bid, employing internally and externally developed computer models. In determining how much to bid, these models often consider the average balance per debt in the portfolio, the average number of months since the creditor charged off the debt, the average number of months since the debtor made the last payment, the states in which the debtors reside, the distribution of balances on the debts, the prevalence of time-barred debts, and the type of accounts being sold. Potential buyers also may consider their past revenues and expenses in purchasing and collecting on comparable portfolios. Because debt buyers compete with each other in bidding on portfolios, they consider the precise methods they use to determine what to bid on portfolios to be proprietary and highly confidential.

Buyers also may use the information provided in a seller's survey, such as how many third-party collectors tried to collect on the debts on behalf of the creditors before or after the creditors charged off the debts. In addition, buyers may also consider their own experience with different collection strategies, the availability and cost of information about the debts, and the potential resale value of the portfolio. Some debt buyers

---

93   Sellers often require potential purchasers to execute confidentiality agreements to obtain bid files. Under these agreements, potential buyers often are required to destroy such materials if they do not purchase the portfolios.

94   Seller surveys also appear to be less common in portfolios of debt for which the debtors have declared bankruptcy.

reported that they also consider factors extrinsic to the portfolio itself, such as the availability of financing and predictions regarding the general economic environment.[95]

D. BUYERS BIDDING ON PORTFOLIOS

Sellers usually establish a specified period of time for prospective purchasers to evaluate portfolios and submit their bids. Prospective purchasers generally make an offer expressed as a percentage of the outstanding principal balance of debts in the portfolio (*e.g.*, 5% on $1,000,000 in debt), but they also can make an offer expressed as a specific sum (*e.g.*, $50,000). In determining the outstanding principal balance of the debts in the portfolio for bid purposes, debt sellers usually exclude interest accrued on debts after the creditors charged off the debt, because collectors rarely are able to recover such interest. At the end of the period of time for bids, debt sellers usually accept the highest bid they receive and inform bidders as to their decision.

E. PRICES BUYERS PAID FOR PORTFOLIOS

The price of debt portfolios has fluctuated over the years depending on the supply of and demand for debt in the marketplace.[96] Based on the information that debt buyers provided in response to its 6(b) orders, the Commission evaluated the relationship between characteristics of debts in portfolios and the prices debt buyers paid for them. The FTC analyzed data for approximately 3,400 portfolios that six going-concern debt buyers not specialized in bankruptcy debt purchased between July 1, 2006 and June 30, 2009. These portfolios contained nearly 76 million debt accounts (*i.e.*, individual consumer debts). Full details on the data and statistical methods used for this analysis are provided in **Technical Appendix B**.

Table 6 presents the average or "mean" characteristics of debt accounts purchased by these six debt buyers. **Table 6** breaks down these mean characteristics based on the type of debt seller, that is, original creditors, resellers, and all sources.

---

95   The information that debt buyers in the Commission's study said that they considered generally was consistent with what ACA recommends that its debt buyer members consider before bidding on portfolios. ACA INT'L, *supra* note 92, at 16-18; ACA INT'L, DUE DILIGENCE GUIDELINES 6-13 (2d ed. 2009).

96   *See, e.g.*, Andrews, *supra* note 42, at 8 (reporting that debt prices rose from 2004 to 2007 as demand increased, in large part because buyers often were seeing returns of approximately three times the prices paid); *Bad Debt Prices Soar as Supply Slows*, COLLECTIONS & CREDIT RISK, Sept. 2010; *Bad-Debt Market Prices Up, Supply Down*, COLLECTIONS & CREDIT RISK, June 2011 (debt buyers were paying 10 cents on the dollar or more for the freshest accounts, depending on the type of portfolio, in large part because the supply of available debt remained low because of tighter credit standards that lenders imposed); Bill Grabarek, *How Low Can They Go?*, CARDS & PAYMENT SOURCE, Oct. 1, 2009, at 20 (price of newly charged-off credit card debt dropped from as much as 14 cents per dollar of debt in early 2008 to between 4 and 7 cents per dollar as of August 2009); *Investors Return to Debt Buying; Prices Still High*, COLLECTIONS & CREDIT RISK, July 2010, at 21 (prices increased in 2010 as a result of improved economic conditions and a reduction in the supply of debt as creditors significantly reduced the number of credit cards they issued in 2008 and 2009).

Debt buyers in the sample acquired the vast majority of debts (a little over 80 percent) from the original creditor, almost 40 percent of which were credit card debts.[97] Medical and telecommunication debts also comprised a considerable share of the debts that the buyers acquired from original creditors. A little over a quarter of the debts acquired from original creditors had a face value greater than one thousand dollars.

On average, debt buyers paid 4.0 cents for each dollar of debt.[98] It is important to note, however, that although the price paid by debt buyers for debts is low relative to their face value, it does not necessarily follow that the profit from collecting on those debts will be high.[99] First, debt buyers do not recover the face value of all of the debts that they purchase. Debt buyers typically do not attempt collections on all accounts they purchase,[100] do not usually realize recoveries on every account for which collections are attempted,[101] and do not typically recover the full face value on accounts for which they do realize recoveries. Second, debt buyers, like any other debt collectors, also incur substantial costs in collecting on debts.

The FTC also conducted a regression analysis to determine what factors influenced the price at which debt sellers sold portfolios to debt buyers.[102] **Table 7** presents the results of that analysis. The regression model predicts that debt considered as "baseline debt" for purposes of the analysis had an average price of 7.9 cents per dollar of outstanding debt balance. The baseline corresponds to a credit card debt that is less than 3 years old, acquired from the original creditor, with a face value less than one thousand dollars, and that had never been sent to a contingency collector.[103]

As shown in **Table 7**, debt buyers generally paid less for older debts than for newer ones. The FTC's analysis suggests that debt buyers paid on average 3.1 cents per dollar of debt for debts that were 3 to 6 years old and 2.2 cents per dollar of debt for debts that were 6 to 15 years old compared to 7.9 cents per dollar for

---

97 These and other figures in Table 6 represent percentages of debt accounts. Figures presented earlier in this report showing credit card debt comprising a higher percentage of all sold debt were based on percentages of total portfolios, face values, and expenditures.

98 This figure was derived from the sample of portfolios used in the regression analysis, described below. The average price for all portfolios submitted to the FTC was 4.5 cents per dollar of debt. The Commission's estimate of the prices paid on average for debts generally is consistent with other estimates of debt prices. *See, e.g.*, Hunt, *supra* note 71, at 11 ("Average price of $1 in bad [credit] cards loans was 5.3 cents [in 2006].").

99 In 2007, ACA International stated that debt buyers expected at that time to recover 2.5 times what they paid to acquire accounts over a period of five years. Andersen & Beato, *supra* note 33, at 41. Debt buyers' expenses, of course, would have to be deducted from these revenues to determine the profit that debt buyers realize.

100 For example, Encore stated the following in its 2008 annual report: "We use our collection resources judiciously and efficiently by not deploying resources on accounts where the prospects of collection are remote. For example, for accounts where the debtor is currently unemployed, overburdened by debt, incarcerated, or deceased, no collection method of any sort is assigned." Encore Capital Group, *supra* note 75, at 4.

101 TERP & BOWNE, *supra* note 44, at 3 ("[Debt] buyers hope to make a profit by collecting at least a small percentage of [the accounts they purchase].").

102 Regression analysis is a statistical technique for estimating the relationship between one or more "explanatory" variables, such as the age and type of debt, and a "dependent" variable, such as the price of debt. More specifically, the regression analysis shows how price varies when any one of the explanatory variables changes, holding the other explanatory variables constant.

103 All of the other reported coefficient estimates in **Table 7** should be interpreted as the predicted difference in debt price relative to this baseline type of debt.

debts less than 3 years old.[104] Finally, debt buyers paid effectively nothing for accounts that were older than fifteen years. Debt buyers presumably pay less for older debts because their expected return from collecting on those debts is lower, likely reflecting the fact that the consumers may be less willing or able to pay the debt or the consumers may be more difficult for debt buyers to locate.

The amount purchasers paid for debts also varied by the type of debt. As shown in **Table 7**, relative to credit card debt, the debt buyers paid substantially more for mortgage debt and significantly less for debts such as medical and utility debt.[105] The debt buyers, on average, also paid less for debts for which sellers previously hired third-party collectors to try to recover and for debts for which there was no information, or incomplete information, about third-party collection attempts. Unsuccessful third-party collection efforts may indicate a lower probability of collection, and likely explain why debt buyers are not as willing to pay as much for these debts. Similarly, debt buyers may be wary of debt for which the seller has not disclosed whether previous collection activities occurred, because these debts may have been subject to unsuccessful collection efforts.

The regression analysis did not find any statistically significant differences between the prices paid for debt purchased from resellers versus debt purchased from original creditors, once one controls for the other characteristics of the debt. This suggests that the difference in the average sales prices of debt from the two types of sellers is due to differences in the age, type, and previous collection history of debts sold, rather than the type of seller.[106]

F. CONTRACTUAL AGREEMENTS TO PURCHASE DEBT

Once a debt seller has decided to accept a debt buyer's bid on a portfolio, the two parties enter into a purchase and sale agreement to consummate the deal. The debt buyers in the Commission's study submitted a substantial number of purchase and sale agreements for the FTC's review. A comprehensive discussion of these contracts and their terms is set forth in **Technical Appendix C**. This section provides an abbreviated version of the information in the appendix, with a particular emphasis on the terms of purchase and sale agreements that might affect the transfer of information about debts from debt sellers to debt buyers.

Although debt sellers and debt buyers are both parties to purchase and sale agreements, sellers generally appear to draft them. Each debt buyer in the study submitted purchase and sale agreements with a variety of structures, organization, and phrasing. Where different debt buyers entered into purchase and sale

---

104 This pattern of prices across different types of debt is consistent with what the FTC has found in its law enforcement investigations.

105 The substantially higher price for mortgage debt may be due to the fact that mortgage debt is generally secured by real property and because debt buyers included some portfolios of mortgages on which consumers were current with their payments.

106 *See infra* **Technical Appendix B** at p. B-9; *see also* GLOBAL DEBT BUYING, *supra* note 38, at 25("[T]he price of a debt portfolio is directly related to the age of the portfolio and the number of times that the underlying accounts have been worked by other collection agencies.").

agreements with the same seller, however, the structure, organization, and phrasing of these agreements were virtually identical. In general, the only differences among these agreements were the quantity of the debts in the portfolio and the prices paid. Debt sellers thus appear to be responsible for many of the terms and conditions governing the sale of debt.

The purchase and sale agreements typically defined the type of debt being sold in terms of broad debt categories (*e.g.*, credit cards, loans, medical debts, etc.) and descriptors of past collection activities, such as the number of times the owners of the debts had placed them with contingency and other third-party collectors. The description of debt portfolios in purchase and sale agreements was consistent with how sellers describe portfolios when they are created, marketed, and advertised to debt buyers.

Debt sale contracts determine how debts and information about them pass from debt sellers to debt buyers. Some contract features may also affect: (1) information debt buyers receive about the debts they purchase; (2) remedies available to debt buyers in the event that purchased accounts lack accurate information or may not be collectable; (3) how debt buyers interact with consumers; and (4) the resale of purchased debts to other debt buyers.

In many purchase and sale agreements, sellers disclaimed all warranties and representations regarding the accuracy of the information they provided at the time of sale about individual debts, essentially selling the debts, with some limited exceptions, "as is." Contracts typically gave debt buyers some refund, or "put-back," rights when purchased debts did not have the attributes necessary to be included in the portfolio of debts sold. For example, debt buyers typically could put back "ineligible accounts" to debt sellers that included debts owed by consumers who had died or who had declared bankruptcy on or before a specific date prior to the transfer of ownership to the debt buyer. Purchase and sale agreements tended to provide debt buyers with a relatively easy and low cost means of providing proof that a consumer had died or entered bankruptcy prior to the specified date.[107]

In contrast, most purchase and sale agreements provided very limited, if any, right for debt buyers to put back debts to debt sellers on the grounds that information from debt sellers about individual debts was missing or inaccurate. As noted above, contracts commonly stated that debts were sold "as is and with all faults." However, the fact that debts were generally sold "as is" does not necessarily mean that errors or inaccuracies were or were not prevalent.[108] The study did not test the accuracy of the information conveyed by debt sellers to debt buyers. Accordingly, the study does not permit any conclusions to be drawn as to the prevalence of errors or inaccuracies in debts generally sold "as is."

---

107 Put-back rights also were extended to debts that were the result of fraud or whose balances included amounts attributable to fraud. The documentation that debt sellers required for these debts to be put back appears to have been less consistent but generally more rigorous than the documentation required for debt buyers to put back debts because of death or bankruptcy.

108 There may be other reasons why debt information generally is not warranted. For example, it may be costly for sellers to determine whether each returned debt was truly inaccurate or simply had been uncollectible for the buyer.

Purchase and sale agreements for debt portfolios typically put limitations on the rights of debt buyers to acquire copies of documents associated with creating and servicing debts included in the portfolios. Debt buyers often were given a defined amount of time (typically between six months and three years) to request a defined maximum number of documents at no charge.[109] Some contracts also limited the frequency with which debt buyers could submit requests to obtain document copies. After the period for debt buyers to receive information at no cost ended, or after debt buyers had obtained the maximum number of free copies, whichever came first, the debt sale contracts specified the price (usually between five and ten dollars and sometimes higher per document) and quantity of documents that debt buyers had the option of purchasing. Purchase and sale agreements also often specified a time after which debt buyers would no longer be able to exercise this option. Debt sellers under these contracts often had substantial time, typically up to sixty days, to comply with requests from debt buyers for documents.

Contracts typically also included some terms and conditions regulating each party's post-sale interactions with consumers. These restrictions could make it more difficult for consumers to learn that original creditors sold their debts to others or to learn of the origins of debts that debt buyers are attempting to collect from them. No contracts required credit issuers (or subsequent resellers) to notify consumers that their debts had been sold to a debt buyer. Further, debt buyers were often restricted in how they could use the names of the original creditors (or other debt sellers) in communications with debtors.[110] For example, some contracts expressly prohibited debt buyers from using the original creditor or other seller's name in the subject line of letters sent to consumers.[111] And contracts often prohibited debt buyers from giving consumers (even in response to in-bound calls or letters from consumers) contact information for the original creditor or other debt seller, which likely means that debt buyers were prohibited from sharing the specialized credit issuer contact information they acquired as a result of the sale (*i.e.*, the name, phone number, fax number, mailing address, etc.) of any of the seller's employees or divisions that served as a contact point for the debt buyer. Debt buyers, however, were not prohibited from providing consumers with the official postal address of the original creditor, possibly because Section 809(b) of the FDCPA requires debt collectors to provide consumers with the name and address of the original creditor if consumers request that information.[112]

Most contracts contained terms addressing actions the original creditor or other debt seller would take if it received consumer payments for debts that had been sold. If the debt seller was a bank selling debts arising from credit it had extended, contracts often permitted a lag of sixty days between the bank's receipt of the consumer's payment and the forwarding of that payment to the debt buyer. Some contracts also

---

109 The maximum number of copies was often specified in terms of a percentage of debts sold, typically between 10% and 25% of the number of accounts sold.

110 The Commission has recommended that the FDCPA be modified to require that the validation notice include the original creditor's name. CHALLENGES OF CHANGE, *supra* note 1, at 26.

111 A few contracts that the FTC evaluated related to portfolios of co-branded credit card debts, and these typically prohibited debt buyers from referring to the co-branded entities in any written communications to consumers and limited the mention of the co-branded entities to telephonic communications with consumers.

112 15 U.S.C. § 1692g(b) (2006).

provided that banks would not reduce the amount forwarded to the debt buyer as a service fee for an initial period of time, but allowed the deduction of service fees after that period.[113] None of the contracts required banks receiving consumer payments on debts that had been sold to notify consumers that their payments had been forwarded to debt buyers. Delays in forwarding payments and the fees deducted for doing so could result in delayed posting of payments to accounts and discrepancies between the amounts that consumers and debt buyers believed had been paid on debts.[114]

The FTC did not receive any contracts that were written specifically to sell debts that were beyond the statute of limitations. Although some contracts permitted debt buyers to put back out-of-statute debts, most were either silent about out-of-statute debts or expressly stated that sellers' inclusion of out-of-statute debts was not a breach of the contract.[115]

The debt buyers in the study asserted that they use purchase and sale agreements in reselling debts that are substantially similar to the agreements they enter into when purchasing debts from original creditors. The FTC's review of the purchase and sale agreements that these resellers produced corroborates this assertion. Some contracts between debt sellers and debt buyers expressly prohibited debt buyers from reselling any of the debts acquired under the contract, or placed restrictions on when and to whom the debt buyer could resell the debts. More commonly, however, contracts permitted debt buyers to resell debts, but required either that the original debt seller pre-approve the resale or that the debt buyer notify the debt seller prior to resale. Virtually all contracts that permitted debt buyers to resell debts required that they state in their contracts with purchasers of the resold debts that: (1) the purchasers of the resold debts were subject to the terms and conditions of the original purchase and sale agreements; and (2) the original sellers had no obligations to the purchasers of the resold debts. In particular, original sellers had no obligation to provide copies of documents directly to purchasers of resold debts; instead, these purchasers were required to forward

---

113 Contracts where sellers were not depository banks, however, generally reflected faster transmission of consumer payments. Service fees for forwarding payments to debt buyers also were relatively uncommon in contracts for debts other than credit card accounts.

114 It should be noted, however, that the Commission has no information on how frequently consumers sent payments to credit issuers instead of the debt buyers that had purchased their accounts, nor whether banks customarily took the full time lag permitted to them when forwarding such payments to debt buyers. Likewise, the FTC lacks information on the significance of such delays, and the reduction in consumer payments due to forwarding bank service, in comparison to other probable causes of "wrong amount" account balances.

115 Note that to resolve allegations that a debt buyer made deceptive claims in seeking to collect on time-barred debt, the consent order in *Asset Acceptance* imposed restrictions on the debt buyer's resale of time-barred debt, including prohibiting the sale, transfer, or assignment of the right to commence any arbitration or legal action to recover on any time-barred debt for which the buyer had made order-mandated disclosures. Consent Decree at 13-14, *United States v. Asset Acceptance, LLC*, No. 8:12-cv-00182 (M.D. Fla. Jan. 31, 2012), *available at* http://www.ftc.gov/opa/2012/01/asset.shtm.

any requests through the original purchaser.[116] Original sellers also did not typically accept "put-backs" of ineligible debts from buyers of resold debt.[117]

Some contracts for the resale of debt indicated that debt buyers reselling debts charged additional fees or added transmittal time when passing copies of document requests and documents up and down the chain between purchasers of resold debts and the original seller. The time and cost involved in obtaining these copies may create a disincentive for requesting them, including in situations where such information would be useful to debt buyers in verifying disputed debts.

---

116 Similarly, if the original credit issuer, or any subsequent owner of a debt, received a consumer payment on a debt they no longer owned, contracts typically required only that the recipient forward the payment to the party to whom they sold the debt, even if that party no longer owned the debt.

117 Note, however, that some debt buyers extended additional put-back rights binding themselves, but not the original credit issuer, when they resold debt.

VI. INFORMATION IN THE COLLECTION PROCESS

Debt buyers acquire, evaluate, and use information about debts and debtors throughout the process of collecting on debts. Debt buyers may obtain this information from sellers, third-parties, consumers, and others. If debt buyers have sufficient and accurate information about debts, they are more likely to recover on them.[118] Debt buyers therefore have an incentive to pay for information about debts so long as the benefit from a greater likelihood of recovery exceeds the cost of the information.

In recent years, serious concerns have been raised about the sufficiency and accuracy of the information that debt buyers have at all stages of the collection process. Consumer groups have said that debt buyers typically receive from debt sellers at the time of sale only an electronic spreadsheet containing minimal information about debts and debtors.[119] They also have charged that debt buyers often do little or nothing to verify debts if consumers dispute their validity – that is, they do not conduct an adequate investigation of consumer claims that they are not the debtor or that the amount of the debt being collected is incorrect.[120]

The Commission's enforcement actions and its policy work reflect similar concerns. For example, in its 2012 action against debt buyer Asset Acceptance, the FTC alleged that the company failed to adequately verify disputed debts.[121] And in its 2009 report on debt collection, the Commission underscored the importance of data accuracy and debt verification for debt buyers and other debt collectors.[122] The FTC also has brought numerous actions against debt collectors alleging that they made unsubstantiated claims that consumers owed debts or the amount of these debts, in violation of Section 5 of the FTC Act.[123]

---

118 Emily Grace, *Documentation Dilemmas*, COLLECTOR, Nov. 2010, at 22 ("As collectors, we'd love to have better documentation. It would only increase recoveries." (quoting Dan Buell, vice president, Experian)); *see also* GLOBAL DEBT BUYING, *supra* note 38, at 134 ("[I]f a seller provides a lot of data, buyers will become more efficient, and this benefits both buyers and sellers." (quoting Stacey Schacter, CEO, EMCC)).

119 HOBBS & WU, *supra* note 44, at 4; 1 NAT'L CONSUMER LAW CTR., FAIR DEBT COLLECTION § 1.5.4.5 (7th ed. 2011); TERP & BOWNE, *supra* note 44, at 7.

120 *See* Nat'l Consumer Law Ctr. & Nat'l Ass'n of Consumer Advocates, Comments for the FTC Debt Collection Workshop 12-13 (June 6, 2007), *available at* http://www.ftc.gov/os/comments/debtcollectionworkshop/529233-00018.pdf.

121 *United States v. Asset Acceptance, LLC*, No: 8:12-cv-00182 (M.D. Fla. Jan. 31, 2012), *available at* http://www.ftc.gov/opa/2012/01/asset.shtm (debt collector settled allegations that it violated the FTC Act by lacking a reasonable basis for representing to borrowers that they owed a debt (1) when the debt collector had reason to believe certain portfolios contained unreliable data and (2) after the borrowers disputed the debt); *see also United States v. Allied Interstate, Inc.*, No. 0:10-cv-04295 (D. Minn. Oct. 21, 2010), *available at* http://www.ftc.gov/opa/2010/10/alliedinterstate.shtm (debt collector settled allegations that it violated Section 5 of the FTC Act by lacking a reasonable basis for representing to borrowers that they owed a debt after the borrowers disputed the debt); *United States v. Credit Bureau Collection Servs.*, No. 2:10-cv-169 (S.D. Ohio Feb. 24, 2010), *available at* http://www.ftc.gov/opa/2010/03/creditcollect.shtm (debt collector settled allegations that it violated Section 5 of the FTC Act by lacking a reasonable basis for representing to borrowers that they owed a debt); *FTC v. EMC Mortg. Corp.*, No. 4:08-cv-338 (E.D. Tex. Sept. 9, 2008), *available at* http://www.ftc.gov/opa/2008/09/emc.shtm (mortgage servicer settled allegations that it violated Section 5 of the FTC Act by lacking a reasonable basis for representations that it made to borrowers, including claims about the unpaid principal amount, the due date, the interest rate, the delinquency status, and fees and corporate advances that prior mortgage loan servicers had assessed).

122 CHALLENGES OF CHANGE, *supra* note 1, at 30-34.

123 *See infra* note 134 and accompanying text.

Similarly, the Commission, consumer advocates, and academics have issued studies, reports, and articles questioning the sufficiency and accuracy of the information and documentation supporting the complaints debt buyers file in court,[124] and advocating changes in such information and documentation.[125] Private actions similarly have challenged the sufficiency and accuracy of the information that debt buyers have offered to prove that consumers owed debts.[126] And state courts and attorneys general have issued rules increasing the pleading requirements of debt buyers, and sometimes other debt collectors, initiating debt collection litigation.[127] These developments are intended to provide sufficient information for consumers to defend themselves in court, and for courts to evaluate the merits of debt collection complaints.

As part of this study, the FTC undertook an extensive evaluation of the information that debt buyers obtain and use in connection with collecting debts.

A. LEGAL REQUIREMENTS FOR INFORMATION THAT COLLECTORS MUST HAVE AND USE IN COLLECTING ON DEBTS

Federal law establishes minimum requirements for the information debt collectors must have at various times during the collection process. Section 809(a) of the FDCPA requires that collectors provide consumers with a written "validation notice," with information about the debt, within five days after their initial communication with consumers. The validation notice must contain (1) the amount of the debt; (2) the name of the current owner of the debt; and (3) statements explaining, among other things, the

---

124 *See, e.g.*, REPAIRING A BROKEN SYSTEM, *supra* note 3, at iii, 16-17; ROBERT MARTIN, DIST. COUNCIL 37 MUN. EMPS. LEGAL SERVS., WHERE'S THE PROOF? WHEN DEBT BUYERS ARE ASKED TO SUBSTANTIATE THEIR CLAIMS IN COLLECTION LAWSUITS AGAINST NYC EMPLOYEES AND RETIREES, THEY DON'T 3 (2009) [hereinafter WHERE'S THE PROOF?], *available at* http://www. dc37.net/benefits/health/pdf/MELS_proof.pdf (New York legal services provider found that debt buyers provided proof of the debt in only 5.5% of the cases in which proof was requested); TERP & BOWNE, *supra* note 44, at 7; Holland, *supra* note 40; Spector, *supra* note 40, at 291-92 (in more than 95% of 507 collection lawsuits that debt buyers filed in Dallas County, Texas, the complaints failed to provide any information regarding the date of default or a breakdown of the amount owed by principal, interest, and fees).

125 *See* GAO FDCPA REPORT, *supra* note 43.

126 *See, e.g.*, Class Action Complaint at 3-8, *Vassalle v. Midland Funding LLC*, No. 3:11-CV-00096 (N.D. Ohio Jan. 17, 2011) (challenging practice of "robo-signing" affidavits used in debt collection lawsuits); *see also Midland Funding LLC v. Brent*, 644 F. Supp. 2d 961, 966-69 (N.D. Ohio 2009) (describing the challenged affidavit production practice). Note that the FTC filed an amicus brief in the Midland lawsuit opposing a proposed settlement because it provided only a small payment to consumers (capped at $10), and consumers would surrender their rights under the FDCPA and state laws to challenge Midland's actions related to the company's use of affidavits in debt collection lawsuits. FTC's Brief as Amicus Curiae, *Vassalle v. Midland Funding LLC*, No: 3:11-CV-00096 (N.D. Ohio June 21, 2011), *available at* http://www.ftc. gov/os/2011/06/110621midlandfunding.pdf. The court ultimately approved the settlement agreement in *Midland* without making changes to the agreement. *Vassalle v. Midland Funding LLC*, No: 3:11-CV-00096, 2011 WL 3557045 (N.D. Ohio Aug. 12, 2011).

127 *See, e.g.*, MD. R. 3-306(d) (Sept. 8, 2011) (requiring debt buyers to submit a series of documents and information when seeking a judgment by affidavit, including documents establishing the existence of the account and the chain of title, and an itemization of the debt); Admin. Directive, No. 2011-1, *Consumer Debt Collection Actions* ¶ 1 (Del. Ct. C.P. Mar. 16, 2011), *available at* http://www.courts.delaware.gov/CommonPleas/docs/AD2011-1ConsumerDebt0.pdf (requiring all debt collection complaints to include, among other things, the name of the original creditor, the full chain of the assignment of the debt, and an itemized accounting of the amount due).

right of consumers under the FDCPA to dispute debts and to request the name and the address of the original creditor, if different from the creditor that owns the debt. To ensure that consumers have sufficient information about debts, the FTC has recommended that Congress amend Section 809(a) to require that validation notices also include: (1) the name of the original creditor; (2) an itemization of the principal, total interest, and total fees that make up the debt; and (3) two additional statements notifying consumers of two significant rights they have under the FDCPA.[128]

After a debt collector provides a consumer with a validation notice, Section 809(b) of the FDCPA gives consumers the right to dispute the debt. Pursuant to Section 809(a)(4), the validation notice must disclose to consumers that they have thirty days to dispute the debt and that their dispute must be in writing. For example, a consumer may contend that the collector is trying to collect from the wrong person or collect the wrong amount. If a consumer notifies a debt collector, in writing, within thirty days after receipt of a validation notice that he or she is disputing the debt, the collector must discontinue collecting on the debt (or the disputed portion of the debt) until the collector obtains "verification" of the debt and mails it to the consumer. Among other things, Congress intended Section 809(b) to address the problem of debt collectors collecting from the wrong person, the wrong amount, or both.[129]

In its 2009 Debt Collection Workshop Report, the Commission found that many debt collectors respond to verification requests simply by confirming that the demand for payment is consistent with the information in the collector's possession and then informing consumers in writing that they have verified the debt.[130] The FTC determined that a more substantial investigation of disputed debts was consistent with and would further the Congressional intent behind Section 809(b).[131] In particular, the Commission concluded that the FDCPA should be amended to clarify that collectors must conduct reasonable investigations that are responsive to the specific disputes consumers have raised to verify debts.[132] The information that is responsive to these specific disputes will vary, but it is likely to involve obtaining and evaluating information beyond the limited information that sellers provide to debt buyers at the time of sale. For example, assume that a consumer's telephone number is correct in the records of an original creditor but the creditor transposes the last two digits of the number in the documents it provides to a debt buyer. If a recipient of the call from the debt buyer disputes the debt, the debt buyer would not discover the error

---

128 CHALLENGES OF CHANGE, *supra* note 1, at 26. The consumer rights are contained in two FDCPA sections: FDCPA § 809(b), 15 U.S.C. § 1692g(b) (2006), which provides that, if a consumer disputes a debt or requests verification of the debt in writing within thirty days of receiving the validation notice, the debt collector must suspend collection efforts until it obtains verification of the debt and mails it to the consumer; and FDCPA § 805(c), 15 U.S.C. § 1692c(c), which requires a debt collector to cease contacting a consumer about a debt if the consumer so requests in writing.

129 S. REP. No. 95-382, at 4 (1977), *reprinted in* 1977 U.S.C.C.A.N. 1695, 1699; *see also Chaudhry v. Gallerizzo*, 174 F.3d 394, 406 (4th Cir. 1999) (purpose of verification is to prevent debt collectors from "dunning the wrong person or attempting to collect debts which the consumer has already paid").

130 CHALLENGES OF CHANGE, *supra* note 1, at 32.

131 *Id.*

132 *Id.* at 33.

if it only checks the documents it received from the original creditor, but it would discover the error if it reviewed the original creditor's records.

In addition to the FDCPA, debt collectors also must comply with Section 5 of the FTC Act. A collector that makes an objective claim to a consumer without a "reasonable basis" for it engages in deception in violation of Section 5 of the FTC Act. [133] Debt collectors make express or implied representations at many stages of the collection process that particular consumers owe debts in a specific amount. For instance, during a phone call with a consumer a debt collector might state "I am collecting the $1,000 you owe on your credit card." The FTC has emphasized in numerous law enforcement actions[134] and policy pronouncements[135] in recent years that debt collectors that do not have adequate support for such representations are engaged in deception in violation of Section 5 of the FTC Act.

The Commission has explained that whether a debt collector has a reasonable basis for a claim that the consumer owes a debt is a very fact-specific inquiry.[136] In particular, whether a debt collector has information to substantiate the claim generally will depend, in part, on when in the collection process the collector makes the claim.[137] The FTC has explained that, "[i]n many situations, the account information that a debt collector receives from the owner of the debt may provide a reasonable basis for asserting that a consumer owes the debt, even if the debt collector has attempted to collect from the wrong consumer or to

---

133 Federal Trade Commission Policy Statement Regarding Advertising Substantiation, *appended to In re Thompson Med. Co.*, 104 F.T.C. 648, 839 (1984), *aff'd*, 791 F.2d 189 (D.C. Cir. 1986). The Statement sets forth the requirement, articulated in prior Section 5 cases, that advertisers must have a reasonable basis for making objective claims before the claims are disseminated. *Id.*

134 *See, e.g., United States v. Luebke Baker & Assocs.*, No. 1:12-cv-01145 (C.D. Ill. May 23, 2012), *available at* http://www.ftc. gov/opa/2012/05/luebkenr.shtm (debt collector settled allegations that it violated Section 5 of the FTC Act by lacking a reasonable basis for representing to borrowers that they owed a debt); *United States v. Asset Acceptance, LLC*, No: 8:12-cv-00182 (M.D. Fla. Jan. 31, 2012), *available at* http://www.ftc.gov/opa/2012/01/asset.shtm (debt collector settled allegations that it violated the FTC Act by lacking a reasonable basis for representing to borrowers that they owed a debt (1) when the debt collector had reason to believe certain portfolios contained unreliable data and (2) after the borrowers disputed the debt); *United States v. Allied Interstate, Inc.*, No. 0:10-cv-04295 (D. Minn. Oct. 21, 2010), *available at* http://www.ftc.gov/ opa/2010/10/alliedinterstate.shtm (debt collector settled allegations that it violated the FTC Act by lacking a reasonable basis for representing to borrowers that they owed a debt after the borrowers disputed the debt); *United States v. Credit Bureau Collection Servs.*, No. 2:10-cv-169 (S.D. Ohio Feb. 24, 2010), *available at* http://ftc.gov/opa/2010/03/creditcollect. shtm (debt collector settled allegations that it violated the FTC Act by lacking a reasonable basis for representing to borrowers that they owed a debt); *FTC v. EMC Mortg. Corp.*, No. 4:08-cv-00338 (E.D. Tex. Sept. 9, 2008), *available at* http://www.ftc.gov/opa/2008/09/emc.shtm (mortgage servicer settled allegations that it violated the FTC Act by lacking a reasonable basis for representations made to borrowers, including claims about the unpaid principal amount, due date, interest rate, delinquency status, and fees and corporate advances that prior mortgage loan servicers had assessed); *see also FTC v. Countrywide Home Loans, Inc.*, No. 2-10-cv-04193 (C.D. Cal. June 7, 2010), *available at* http://www.ftc.gov/ opa/2010/06/countrywide.shtm (mortgage servicer settled allegations that it violated the FTC Act by lacking a reasonable basis for representations made to borrowers in bankruptcy, including claims about amounts owed for pre-petition arrearage and the amount and delinquency status of post-petition payments).

135 *See, e.g.,* CHALLENGES OF CHANGE, *supra* note 1, at 2, 24-25.

136 *Id.* at 25.

137 *Id.*

collect the wrong amount."[138] Indeed, in certain circumstances, it may be reasonable to rely on information received from the creditor that sold the debt. The Commission also has emphasized, however, that once a consumer has informed the debt collector that he or she does not owe a debt, or does not owe the amount claimed, the collector is likely to need more information before once again claiming that the consumer owes the debt.[139]

In addition to FDCPA and the FTC Act requirements,[140] state laws also impose standards that debt collectors must meet when they file a complaint in court to recover on a debt through the litigation process.[141] Most complaints filed to collect on debts are filed in state courts, and, therefore, state laws, regulations, and rules largely govern what information debt buyers need to have and provide with their complaints when they decide to commence litigation.

In 2010, the Commission reported that the system for resolving consumer debt disputes through litigation was seriously flawed.[142] Among other problems, the FTC found that debt collection complaints often do not contain sufficient information to allow consumers to admit or deny the allegations and assert affirmative defenses.[143] The Commission recommended that states consider requiring that debt collection complaints include the following information: (1) the name of the original creditor and the last four digits of the original account number; (2) the date of default or charge-off and the amount due at that time; (3) the name of the current owner of the debt; (4) the total amount currently due on the debt; and (5) a breakdown of the total amount currently due by principal, interest, and fees.[144] In response to the FTC's report,

---

138 *Id.* The Commission, however, has alleged that a debt collector made unsubstantiated claims in violation of Section 5 of the FTC Act in collecting on debts where the collector knew or should have known that the debts it was trying to collect were not valid because of the owner of the debt's deceptive sales practices. Complaint at ¶ 45-47, *United States v. Luebke Baker & Assocs.*, No. 1:12-cv-01145 (C.D. Ill. May 11, 2012), *available at* http://www.ftc.gov/opa/2012/05/luebkenr.shtm.

139 The Commission, for example, has alleged that a debt buyer made unsubstantiated claims to consumers when it did not obtain or review information about individual debts it purchased even after it learned that some portfolios it purchased contained significant amounts of unreliable data, including Social Security numbers, addresses, and other identification information. Complaint at ¶ 49, *United States v. Asset Acceptance, LLC*, No. 8:12-cv-182 (M.D. Fla. Jan. 30, 2012), *available at* http://www.ftc.gov/opa/2012/01/asset.shtm.

140 Note that the FDCPA and Section 5 of the FTC Act apply to the conduct of debt collectors, including attorneys, in collecting on debts, including collecting on them through litigation. *See Heintz v. Jenkins*, 514 U.S. 291, 294 (1995) (holding that the FDCPA applies to lawyers engaged in litigation). Given the problems the Commission has found in debt collection litigation, as discussed below, the application of the FDCPA to such litigation provides important protections for consumers.

141 *See supra* note 127 and accompanying text.

142 Repairing a Broken System, *supra* note 3, at i.

143 *Id.* at 17.

144 *Id.*

several states have enacted or adopted measures requiring that debt collectors or debt buyers include more information about debts and debtors in the complaints they file in litigation.[145]

B. FTC EVALUATION OF DEBT BUYER INFORMATION

The Commission's study obtained and analyzed data from debt buyers concerning the type and amount of information they obtain during the debt collection process. The data the FTC obtained and analyzed, however, are subject to two important limitations. First, the data evaluated did not include information about debt collection litigation actions, and, therefore, the Commission can neither make findings nor offer conclusions as to the sufficiency and accuracy of information debt buyers have or offer in connection with matters in litigation.[146] Second, the study did not directly evaluate the accuracy of the information that debt buyers obtained but instead focused on what types of information debt buyers obtained, as well as when and how they obtained it. Notwithstanding these limitations, the Commission believes that the data it obtained and analyzed provide valuable insights into the relationship between debt buyers and information in the debt collection system. The data also identify some key issues for future study.

1. INFORMATION OBTAINED FROM SELLERS AT TIME OF PURCHASE

In its study, the Commission obtained information from debt buyers concerning the data files and media they received from debt sellers at the time of sale. The FTC was able to analyze the data files for over 5 million accounts that debt sellers transmitted to debt buyers at the time of purchase.[147] As shown in **Table 8**, debt buyers received the following **information about debtors**: (1) over 98% of debt accounts included the name, street address, and social security number of the debtor; (2) 70% set forth the debtor's home telephone number, and 47% and 15% listed work and mobile telephone numbers, respectively; (3) 65% included the debtor's birth date; and (4) less than 1% revealed the debtor's credit score.

In addition, the debt buyers acquired the following **information about the original creditor's account**: (1) 100% of accounts included the original creditor's account number; (2) 10% stated the credit limit on the

---

145 *See, e.g.,* Response of Creditors' Counsel Identified to Delaware Court of Common Pleas Administrative Directive 2011-1 – Consumer Debt Collection Actions 1 (2011), *available at* http://www.courts.delaware.gov/commonpleas/docs/comment2n.pdf (noting that the Delaware Court of Common Pleas stated that the FTC reports were among the sources consulted in drafting an Administrative Directive setting forth pleading and practice requirements in debt collection cases); Standing Comm. on Rules of Practice & Procedure, 171st Report, at 6-7 (2011), *available at* http://www.mdcourts.gov/rules/ruleschanges.html (noting that the FTC's report was among the sources consulted in developing changes in Maryland court rules).

146 Many courts have concluded that the complaints and documentation filed in individual cases were inadequate. *See, e.g., Nelson v. First Nat'l Bank Omaha,* No. A04-579, 2004 WL 2711032 (Minn. Ct. App. Nov. 30, 2004); *MBNA Am. Bank, N.A. v. Nelson,* No. 13777/06, 2007 N.Y. Misc. LEXIS 4317 (N.Y. Civ. Ct. May 24, 2007); *Citibank (SD), N.A. v. Martin,* 807 N.Y.S.2d 284 (N.Y. Civ. Ct. 2005); *Asset Acceptance Corp. v. Proctor,* 804 N.E.2d 975 (Ohio Ct. App. 2004); *Atlantic Credit & Fin., Inc. v. Giuliana,* 829 A.2d 340 (Pa. Super. Ct. 2003); *Chase Bank USA v. Rader,* No. CI-08-01186, 2009 WL 2757904 (Pa. Ct. Common Pleas Mar. 17, 2009); *First Select Corp. v. Grimes,* No. 2-01-257-CV, 2003 WL 151940 (Tex. App. Jan. 23, 2003).

147 This analysis excludes accounts sold to companies that specialize in bankruptcy debt.

account; (3) 62% specified the type of debt; (4) 46% specified the name of the original creditor;[148] and (5) 30% indicated the interest rate charged on the account.

The debt buyers further obtained the following **information about the amounts debtors owed**: (1) 100% of accounts included the outstanding balance; (2) 72% listed the amount the debtor owed at charge-off; (3) 11% stated the principal amount; and (4) 37% listed finance charges and fees.

Finally, the data files contained **information about key dates** relating to the debts: (1) 97% of accounts indicated the date the debtor opened the account: (2) 90% revealed the date the debtor made his or her last payment; (3) 83% stated the date the original creditor charged off the debt; and (4) 35% set forth the date of first default.

The Commission also was able to assess the documentation, or "media," that debt buyers received from debt sellers at the time of purchase in addition to the data files. Debt buyers submitted information on documentation received at the time of purchase for 333 portfolios, containing 3.9 million accounts, purchased during the six-month period from March through August of 2009.[149] Our evaluation of this submission showed that debt buyers received documents at the time of purchase for only a relatively small percentage of these debts. As shown in **Table 9**, the six buyers included in the analysis reported that they had received documents for 12% of the accounts in the portfolios submitted from this period.[150] The debt buyers reported receiving only three types of documents: account statements, received for 6% of accounts, "terms and conditions" documents, also received for 6% of accounts, and account applications documents, received for less than 1% of accounts. Buyers typically received just one type of document per account.[151] The accounts for which documents were received were highly concentrated in particular portfolios. Only 13% of the portfolios contained any account documents, but overall within this set of portfolios, documents

---

148 Although only about half of the accounts identified the original creditor, buyers were likely to receive this information in other ways as well. For example, the identity of the creditor will be obvious in purchases from the creditor. In addition, many contracts specified that the contract between the original creditor and the original buyer be attached to the contract in any subsequent resale. Although the name of the creditor was not included in the data files for many accounts, the FTC believes that buyers will generally know the name of the original creditor when purchasing debt.

149 The information included in the FTC's analysis was submitted by six going-concern debt buyers not specialized to bankruptcy recoveries. Three debt buyers submitted information on the documents received at the time of purchase for all of the portfolios they purchased during this time period. The other three buyers did not have the information readily available, and because of the likely burden of compiling it, were permitted to provide the information for a small sample of the portfolios they purchased during the period. About 52% of the accounts in the portfolios for which the FTC received information were submitted by one buyer, and about 87% were submitted by two buyers.

150 If the data from the debt buyers that submitted only samples of their portfolios are weighted by the total number of accounts purchased in this period, the estimated percentage of accounts for which any document was received at the time of purchase would decrease to 6%.

151 Buyers received more than one type of document for less than 1% of all accounts for which information was provided. Accounts for which account statements were received typically received multiple statements, usually sufficient to show the account statement history extending back for a year or more.

were received for 90% of the accounts.[152] Credit card debt was the most common debt type for which buyers received documents. Of the accounts for which debt buyers received documents, 90% related to credit card debt.

Thus, the Commission's analysis reveals that the debt buyers usually had all the information that the FDCPA currently requires debt buyers to provide consumers in validation notices at the beginning of the collection process – specifically the name of the current creditor (*i.e.*, the debt buyer itself) and the amount of the debt. Buyers also received additional information from sellers, such as the name of the original creditor,[153] the original creditor's account number, the debtor's social security number, the date of last payment, and the date of charge-off. In the Commission's experience, debt collectors, including debt buyers, generally do not provide this information to consumers when they provide consumers with validation notices. If such information (with appropriate truncations to account and social security numbers to protect privacy) is provided to consumers at the time collectors provide validation notices,[154] it might help consumers determine whether they are the debtor and whether the amount of the debt is correct.

The Commission's study also revealed that there were important limitations on the information that debt buyers received at time of sale. Most significantly, debt buyers often did not receive the information needed to break down outstanding balances on accounts into principal,[155] interest, and fees. The FTC has said that debt collectors should be required to include this information in validation notices to assist consumers in determining whether the amount owed is correct. Moreover, as discussed above, when debt buyers received information about debts at the time of sale, sellers generally disclaimed all warranties and representations with respect to the accuracy of this information.

In addition, sellers usually did not include in the data files they provided to buyers at time of sale information about the specifics of the collection history of the individual debts in their portfolios. Sellers may have tried to collect on debts themselves or retained third-party collectors to recover on their behalf. During these collection attempts, collectors may have obtained information to help them locate consumers who have moved, often referred to as "skip-tracing" information; made notes as to their interactions with consumers; received written disputes from consumers; and sought to verify disputed debts. Such information may not have existed for some debts in some portfolios. But even if the sellers or their third-

---

152   If the data from the debt buyers that submitted samples of their portfolios are weighted by the total number of portfolios purchased in this period, the estimated percentage of portfolios in which any document was received at the time of purchase increases to 20% (even though the percentage of accounts decreases, as noted above).

153   As discussed above, although only about half (46%) of the accounts identified the original creditor in the data files buyers received from sellers, buyers were likely to have the original creditor's name from other sources. *See supra* note 148.

154   The Commission has recommended that validation notices include the name of the original creditor. *See* CHALLENGES OF CHANGE, *supra* note 1, at 27-28. It has also recommended that complaints in debt collection cases state the name of the original creditor, the last four digits of the original account number, and the date of default or charge-off. *See* REPAIRING A BROKEN SYSTEM, *supra* note 3, at iii.

155   As discussed above, however, debt buyers obtained information about the amount owed at charge-off for 72% of accounts.

party collectors had received, collected, and retained such information, they did not include it in data files provided to purchasers at the time of sale.

One particularly important aspect of collection history is a debt's dispute history. Based on the FTC's enforcement experience, debt sellers typically do not provide dispute history information to buyers at the time of sale. The dispute history of debts indicates whether consumers disputed them when sellers sought to collect and whether sellers verified them if disputed. Knowing the dispute history of debts could be very relevant to debt buyers in assessing whether consumers in fact owe the debts and whether the amounts of the debts are correct.

The Commission's analysis also reveals that the information that debt buyers conveyed to other debt buyers when debt was resold was very similar to the information that original creditors provided to debt buyers. Resellers conveyed to debt buyers the same type of data file information about specific debts (*e.g.*, consumer name, social security number, original creditor name, account balance, charge-off date, last payment date, and opening date) that they received from original creditors. With respect to media, most resellers[156] appeared to provide debt buyers with the purchase and sale agreement, a bill of sale, and, in some case, documents showing price calculations or additional transaction-specific documents.[157] This suggests that the initial debt buyers generally do not discard[158] any information they receive from the original creditor, but also that they typically do not supplement the information they provide to secondary debt buyers to reflect their experience in collecting on debts.[159]

2 RATE AT WHICH CONSUMERS DISPUTE DEBTS THAT DEBT BUYERS ATTEMPT TO COLLECT

Consumer disputes of debts can provide some insight into how often debt buyers seek to recover from the wrong consumer or recover the wrong amount. As explained in more detail in **Technical Appendix B**, the Commission calculated the dispute rate for a sample of portfolios purchased by the studied debt buyers between July 1, 2006 and June 30, 2009. Only four of the surveyed debt buyers were able to provide data on disputes. Moreover, these four debt buyers provided dispute rate information only for debts that the

---

156 One debt buyer noted that some resellers may provide the debt buyer at the time of resale with an electronic copy of all media in the reseller's possession related to the relevant debts, although the buyer also stated that it obtains the majority of documents about debts through requesting them from the reseller after the time of purchase.

157 For example, for transactions that include debts subject to a bankruptcy proceeding or judgment debts, the reseller may provide the debt buyer with a limited power of attorney to effect the transfer of the debts from the name of the reseller to the name of the debt buyer.

158 Note that information about debtors and debt may become problematic even if no information is lost. For example, with the passage of time, addresses and the telephone numbers of debtors often may become incorrect even if the information from the original creditor is not lost.

159 Consistent with the conclusion that purchasers of debts receive comparable information about these debts regardless of whether the seller is the original creditor or a debt buyer, the Commission conducted a regression analysis that revealed that, after controlling for other debt characteristics, there was no statistically significant relationship between debt price and whether the debt buyer purchased it from the original creditor or a reseller. *See infra* **Table 7**.

debt buyers collected themselves, not on debts that the debt buyers placed with third-party collectors for recovery.[160]

It is also important to note what is meant by the term "dispute" in this context. As discussed above, the FDCPA gives consumers thirty days following the receipt of a validation notice to file a written dispute with collectors. The Commission requested data on both written and oral disputes. As noted below, however, not all debt buyers kept records of oral disputes, and thus the analysis is limited to the information about disputes that the debt buyers were able to provide.

The Commission's analysis shows that consumers disputed 3.2% of the accounts on which debt buyers in the sample attempted to collect. If this 3.2% dispute rate were applied across the entire debt buying industry, it would result in consumers disputing about 1 million debts each year that debt buyers purchased, that is, about 3 million debts during the three-year period the Commission studied.[161]

It is critical to note that the 3.2% dispute rate the FTC calculated may not accurately capture the extent of information problems with debts on which debt buyers are collecting. In fact, on balance, it is likely to understate these problems. First, consumers may not receive validation notices,[162] and even those who receive notices that raise questions and concerns about a debt may not submit disputes to collectors.[163] For example, some consumers may not read or understand the validation notice because it does not identify the original creditor, they may assume it is junk mail, or they find writing a letter to be unduly burdensome. Second, because the only debt buyers in the study were larger debt buyers that purchased many of their debts directly from original creditors, the dispute rate found in the study is not necessarily reflective of the dispute rate in the industry overall, which includes smaller debt buyers and debt buyers that purchase debts

---

160   Debt buyers attempted collection solely by themselves on 26.8% of purchased debts, both by themselves and through third-party collectors on 31.9% of debts, solely through third-party collectors on 29.2% of debts, and did not attempt collections through any means on 12.1%. *See infra* **Table 10**. An analysis of how various debt characteristics affected the likelihood that buyers attempted internal and third-party collection is presented in **Table 11**.

161   The nine debt buyers surveyed by the FTC purchased about 89 million debts over the three-year sample period. These debt buyers accounted for an estimated 76% of industry purchases, as measured by face value of the purchased debt. This implies that about 117 million debts were purchased by the industry over the three-year period, assuming that the average face value per account is similar in the rest of the industry as in the surveyed debt buyers. The total number of relevant accounts is reduced to about 110 million if the two surveyed debt buyers that specialize in purchasing bankruptcy debt, and do not engage in collection efforts directly with consumers, are excluded. Adjusting this figure to also reflect the fact that the surveyed debt buyers that did not specialize in bankruptcy debt attempted collection efforts, either internally or through third-party collectors, on only 87.9% of their purchased debts, yields an estimate of about 96 million debts purchased during the three-year period on which debt buyers attempted collection. Applying the 3.2% dispute rate to this figure yields an estimate of about 3 million disputed debts over the three year period, or about 1 million per year.

162   For instance, a debt buyer may send a validation notice to the consumer's home address as identified by the seller, yet the consumer might not receive it if he has moved.

163   Note that the FDCPA implicitly recognizes that consumers may not dispute debts that are problematic in that Section 809(c) expressly precludes courts from construing a consumer's failure to dispute a debt as an admission that the consumer is liable for the debt. 15 U.S.C. §1692g(c) (2006). However, the FTC's orders asked for written disputes generally, and did not limit those to written disputes in response to FDCPA validation notices. We do not know to what extent, if any, the buyers in the study included non-FDCPA dispute letters (*e.g.*, a letter received more than 30 days after the validation notice) and included them in the dispute numbers they provided in response to the orders.

from other debt buyers. Third, because the information used to determine the dispute rate did not include disputes raised in response to collection efforts of third-party collectors retained by debt buyers[164] and because debt buyers appear more likely to retain third parties to collect on more difficult debts, the exclusion of these debts might well have lowered the dispute rate. Fourth, not all of the debt buyers kept records of oral disputes, which (again) lowers the calculated dispute rate.[165]

On the other hand, there also are reasons the dispute rate might overstate problems with debt buyers' collecting from the wrong consumer or the wrong amount. For example, because the validation notice lists the current owner of the debt (*i.e.*, the debt buyer) rather than the original creditor, consumers may dispute the debts because they have had no dealings with, and thus do not recognize, the debt buyer.[166] Also, consumers may mistakenly dispute the amount of a debt that is actually correct and subsequently verified.

For all of these reasons, the Commission does not believe that the dispute rate can be used as a precise or definitive indicator of the extent of information problems with debt being collected by debt buyers. Nevertheless, even the 3.2% dispute rate the FTC found indicates that debt buyers seek to collect on more than a million debts each year that consumers assert that they do not owe or that they owe in a different amount. This is a significant consumer protection concern. If the dispute rate understates the prevalence of information problems, which is likely, the concern would be even stronger.

Finally, the FTC's analysis revealed that there was no statistically significant relationship between the likelihood that a debt was disputed and a debt's age or face value.[167] The Commission's analysis also did not find any statistically significant difference between dispute rates for debts purchased directly from original creditors and for debts purchased from resellers of debts. Note, however, that this result may not be the case for tertiary or later debt buyers, which were not included in the study.

3. DOCUMENTS DEBT BUYERS OBTAINED FROM SELLERS AFTER PURCHASE

As discussed above, the debt buyers in the FTC study typically received some information about the debts at the time of sale, including the account number, outstanding balance, and basic information about the debtor. Moreover, purchase and sale agreements typically allowed debt buyers to obtain after purchase a certain amount of documentation from debt sellers upon request at no charge. Sellers typically agreed to provide buyers with documents free of charge for between 10% and 25% of the debts purchased, with time to request such media limited to between six months and three years after the date of sale. In addition,

---

164   Of the debts that the studied debt buyers sought to collect, debt buyers sought to collect 26.8% through internal collections, 29.2% through placement with third-party collectors, and 31.9% through both internal collections and placement with third-party collectors.

165   The dispute rate also does not necessarily include all disputes relating to items on consumers' credit reports, including disputes that were made by consumers to a credit reporting agency as opposed to directly to the debt collector.

166   The Commission's recommendation that the name of the original creditor be listed on the validation notice likely would decrease the probability of such disputes arising.

167   *See infra* **Table 12**.

the purchase and sale agreements usually required that debt buyers pay for information about debts that exceeded the amount permitted without charge under the agreements. Debt buyers typically paid a charge (usually between $5 and $10 per document, but sometimes higher) to original creditors for this additional information.

Debt buyers may obtain additional documents after purchase from original creditors for a number of reasons. In some circumstances, they might acquire such documentation to enhance their collections. Debt buyers also might obtain these documents to comply with regulatory requirements, including investigating and verifying debts that consumers have disputed. Debt buyers further might obtain such documentation to include with a complaint or to support their arguments in debt collection litigation. The data in the FTC's study, however, neither permit the Commission to determine why the studied debt buyers acquired additional information nor allow the FTC to determine the percentage of disputed debts or litigated matters for which debt buyers obtained additional information.

The Commission's study does, however, provide insight into the types of additional documentation debt buyers obtained after purchase and how often they obtained it. **Table 13** shows the percentage of accounts for which various types of documents were obtained after purchase, and the percentage of portfolios for which these documents were obtained for any account, based on an analysis of 1,477,720 accounts in 202 portfolios. Debt buyers obtained account statements after purchase for 6% of accounts, account applications for 6% of accounts, and terms and conditions documents for 8% of accounts. Payment history documents and affidavits each were obtained for less than 1% of accounts, as were all other types of documents combined. These findings show that the debt buyers obtained additional documentation for only a relatively small percentage of debts after the time of purchase. Although documents were obtained for only a relatively small percentage of accounts, this percentage was greater than the percentage of accounts that were disputed, though the Commission could not assess whether these documents actually were used for dispute verification. The Commission also generally did not have information on the extent to which buyers may have requested documents that sellers did not provide because the documents were not available.

4. DEBT BUYER VERIFICATION OF DEBTS THAT CONSUMERS DISPUTED

The information submitted in the study further provides insight into debt buyers' verification of debts that consumers have disputed. As shown in **Table 14**, the Commission's analysis of 713,308 disputed debts in 1,853 portfolios revealed that debt buyers reported that they verified 51.3% of the debts that consumers had disputed.[168] In addition, debt buyers reported that they were more likely to verify debts that they had obtained from the original creditor (55.7%) than debts they had acquired from other debt buyers (35.9%). Regression analysis, presented in **Table 15**, indicates that debt buyers were significantly less likely to report verification of disputed medical, telecommunications, and utility debt, as compared to verification of credit

---

168 As is the case with the dispute data, noted above, only four of the debt buyers were able to submit data on their verification of debts.

card debt.[169] Debt buyers also were significantly less likely to verify debt that was more than six years old, as compared to debt less than three years old. The analysis also indicates that debt buyers were less likely to verify debt purchased from resellers rather than original creditors, but this result was only marginally significant.

This finding suggests that debt buyers may have been able to verify a significant percentage of disputed debts (though the verification rate differs by the age and type of debt). The FTC notes two important caveats, however. First, the Commission did not itself determine that these debts were verified, but rather relied on the debt buyers to report whether the debts had been verified.[170] Second, the Commission does not know what the debt buyers in the study actually did to verify disputed debts. As the FTC has explained, "[m]any debt collectors have responded to verification requests by only confirming in writing for consumers that the amount demanded is what the creditor claims is owed." The Commission stated that, rather than conducting such a minimal inquiry, "a more substantial investigation of disputed debts is consistent with and would further the Congressional intent behind Section 809(b)," namely, addressing the "problem of debt collectors collecting from the wrong person, the wrong amount, or both."[171]

The FTC also examined the extent to which debt buyers sold disputed debt. Only two of the surveyed debt buyers provided data on the sale of disputed debt. Overall, these debt buyers sold 2.9% of their disputed debts, including 4.9% of verified disputed debts and 0.8% of unverified disputed debts. For debt purchased from resellers, these debt buyers sold 3.8% of disputed debts, including 9.7% of verified disputed debts and 0.5% of unverified disputed debts.[172] Because the Commission received information from so few debt buyers on this point, further study is needed on this issue.

---

169 Although the verification rate figures presented above in this paragraph are based on information provided by four of the surveyed debt buyers, technical issues limited the sample of the regression analysis to the data provided by three of the debt buyers.

170 Because debt buyers have an obligation under Section 809(b) of the FDCPA, 15 U.S.C. § 1692g(b) (2006), to verify debts that consumers dispute in writing within 30 days of receipt of a validation notice, this creates an incentive for debt buyers to report disputed debts as verified if there is uncertainty as to whether the verification is adequate.

171 CHALLENGES OF CHANGE, *supra* note 1, at 32. Although what is necessary for such an investigation is a fact-specific inquiry, often a reasonable investigation should include obtaining, evaluating, and providing to the consumer more information than the collector used before making its claim that the consumer owes the debt. For example, the following may be relevant to an investigation into whether the contacted consumer is the debtor: (1) identifying information of the debtor (*e.g.*, name, address, birth date, and social security number); (2) credit application; and (3) billing statements. Similarly, the following may be relevant when a consumer disputes the amount of the debt: (1) terms and conditions; (2) billing statements; and (3) pay history. If a consumer disputes the debt buyer's right to collect the debt, information and documents related to the chain of ownership of the debt — such as an affidavit of sale or lien transfer — may be relevant. For any dispute, documents or information voluntarily provided by consumers (*e.g.*, proof of payment) should also be considered by the debt buyer.

172 *See infra* **Table 14**.

VII. THE COLLECTION OF OLDER DEBTS

As original creditors sell their debt to debt buyers, and debt buyers, in turn, resell debts to other debt buyers, the debts being collected inevitably get older. The ageing of debts in the debt buying process raises two main concerns. First, the information that collectors have about these debts may become less accurate over time, making it more likely that collectors will seek to recover from the wrong consumer, recover the wrong amount, or both.[173] Second, collectors may sue or threaten to sue about debts that are time-barred – that is, beyond the applicable statute of limitation.[174] Collecting on time-barred debts without disclosing that the collector cannot sue to recover is deceptive in some circumstances. The information that the Commission obtained and analyzed during the study provides insight on these two concerns.

A. AGE AND ACCURACY OF DEBTS THAT DEBT BUYERS COLLECT

In response to its 6(b) orders, the Commission received information about the mean and standard deviation of the ages of the accounts in each portfolio purchased by the debt buyers. Debt buyers provided the age of the debt at the time they purchased the debt rather than the age of the debt at the subsequent time or times that they attempted collecting on it. Debt buyers also calculated the age of the debt at the time since charge-off rather than the time since default.

The Commission used this information to estimate the proportion of accounts in the following categories based on age at acquisition: three years old or less; three to six years old; six to fifteen years old; over fifteen years old; and unreported age. Most states' statutes of limitations are between three and six years, and no state's statute of limitations is longer than fifteen years.[175] Debt that is less than three years old was presumably not time-barred. Debt between three and six years old was likely a mix of time-barred and non-time barred debt. Most, but not all,[176] debt that was older than six years old at the time of acquisition was likely time-barred. Debt that was over fifteen years old at purchase was generally time-barred.

---

173   *See, e.g.,* Hobbs & Wu, *supra* note 44, at 4 ("As a result of this lack of documentation for sometimes very old debts, debt buyers frequently pursued flawed claims."); Peter A. Holland, *Defending Junk-Debt-Buyer Lawsuits*, Clearinghouse Rev. J. Poverty L. & Pol'y, May-June 2012, at 12, 13-15.

174   Such debt is also known as "stale" debt, or "out of statute" debt.

175   *See* Goldberg, *supra* note 40, at 750 ("Each state imposes a statute of limitations, typically ranging from three to six years, after which a debtor is no longer legally obligated to pay the debt and can have a judgment dismissed in court."); Steven P. Mandell & Stephen J. Rosenfeld, Practicing Law Inst., *Drafting Software Licenses For Litigation, in* Understanding the Intellectual Property License 2009, at 741, 762 (PLI Patents, Copyrights, Trademarks, and Literary Property, Course Handbook Ser. No. 19149, 2009) ("The statute of limitations on actions for breach of a written agreement usually ranges from three to 15 years.").

176   Some states have statutes of limitations that are greater than six years. *See, e.g.,* 735 Ill. Comp. Stat. Ann. 5/13-206 (West 2012) (ten-year limitation in Illinois for written contracts); Ky. Rev. Stat. Ann. § 413.090 (West 2012) (fifteen-year limitation in Kentucky for written contracts); R.I. Gen. Laws Ann. § 9-1-13(a) (West 2012) (ten-year limitation in Rhode Island for written and non-written contracts). In addition, for some debt, the statute of limitations may have been tolled, such as during bankruptcy, or a consumer may have made a partial payment on the debt. *See, e.g.,* 11 U.S.C. § 108(c) (2006) (tolling statute of limitations during pendency of bankruptcy proceedings); Kan. Stat. Ann. § 60-520(a) (West 2012) (restarting state statute of limitations upon part payment).

The Commission's analysis of the data estimates that: (1) 68.2% of the debt that debt buyers in the study purchased was less than three years old at the time it was acquired; (2) 19.3% of the debt was between three and six years old; (3) 11.3% of the debt was between six and fifteen years old; and (4) 0.8% of debt was over fifteen years old at the time of acquisition.[177] As noted above, however, the Commission's study did not include data from small debt buyers, debt buyers that purchase most of their debt from other debt buyers, and debt buyers who were under FTC investigation. In the FTC's law enforcement experience, many purchasers of older debts and debts with larger numbers of past placements with third-party collectors are smaller firms. There also were substantial variations in the average age of accounts across different portfolio types.

The Commission's analysis might suggest that the debt on which debt buyers collect is not old and is generally not beyond the applicable statute of limitations. Two features of the data in the study, however, caution against reaching such a conclusion. First, over 80% of the debt analyzed in the study was debt that debt buyers purchased directly from original creditors, while many debt buyers not in the study purchase their debts from other debt buyers. Because debts purchased from original creditors tend to be newer than debts purchased from other debt buyers, the studied debt buyers may own debts that generally are newer than those of other debt buyers. This is shown by the debts analyzed in the study that were purchased from other debt buyers: (1) 37.9% of the debt purchased from resellers was less than three years old; (2) 32.1% was between three and six years old; (3) 27.5% was between six and fifteen years old; and (4) 2.6% was over fifteen years old.[178] Second, even for the debts in the study, as noted above, their age was calculated based on the age at the time of purchase, not at the time of collection. Because debt buyers may collect on debts for a significant period of time, using the date of purchase will understate the age of debts that they are collecting.

The data the Commission received also provide insight as to whether the collection methods debt buyers used to collect on purchased debt varied by the age of the debt. The FTC evaluated these issues for debts in the age categories mentioned above — less than three years old, between three and six years old, between six and fifteen years old, and over fifteen years old at the time of purchase. Overall, the debt buyers attempted to collect themselves on 58.7% of debt and sent 61.1% of debt to third-party debt collectors.[179] A regression analysis found that debt buyers are more likely to attempt in-house collection for debt three to fifteen years old compared to debt less than three years old, and more likely to send debt to third-party collectors for debt six to fifteen years old, again compared to debt less than three years old.[180] It further found that debt buyers

---

177   *See infra* **Table 6**.

178   *Id.*

179   *See infra* **Table 10**. These figures are not mutually exclusive. Debt collectors attempt to both collect internally and through third party collectors on 31.9% of debts. Debt buyers did not attempt collection through either means on 12.1% of debt.

180   As noted in note 179, *supra*, these results are not mutually exclusive, as debt collectors attempted to collect a significant percentage of debts both internally and through third party collectors.

are less likely to send debts more than 15 years old to third-party collectors compared to debts less than three years old, but that result was only marginally significant.[181]

The FTC also used the data that debt buyers submitted to examine whether the rate at which consumers dispute debts, and the rate at which the debt buyers reported they were able to verify disputed debts, varied with the age of the debt. The FTC's regression analysis found no statistically significant differences in the dispute rate across debts of different ages.[182]

The Commission did find statistically significant differences in the verification rate across debts of different ages. Regression analysis found that for baseline debt, which consisted of debt that was less than three years old, 58.4% of the debt disputed by consumers was verified, but similar disputed debt aged six years or more was verified only 36.1% of the time.[183] The data did not allow the Commission to assess whether debt buyers were less likely to verify disputed older debts because they attempted verification less often or because their attempts to verify such debt were unsuccessful. Moreover, the data do not show whether the debts that the debt buyers self-reported as verified were, in fact, properly verified. These results indicate that debt buyers verify older disputed debts less frequently than newer disputed debts, but they do not reveal why such a difference exists. Further study is needed to examine the reasons for these differences.

B. TIME-BARRED DEBT

A major concern related to debt buying is the conduct of some debt buyers in collecting, threatening to sue, or suing on debt that is time-barred. The FDCPA and the FTC Act impose limitations on the ability of debt collectors, including debt buyers, to engage in such conduct. State laws also are increasingly imposing additional restrictions on collection efforts relating to time-barred debt. Through this study, the Commission sought to determine to what extent debt buyers use various methods to recover on time-barred debt.

Statutes of limitations set a maximum time after the accrual of a cause of action in which a plaintiff may file suit. Statutes of limitations serve a variety of purposes. They reflect the legislative judgment that "it is unjust to fail to put the adversary on notice to defend within a specified period of time."[184] They also are designed to "protect defendants and the courts from having to deal with cases in which the search for truth

---

181   *See infra* **Table 11**.

182   *See infra* **Table 12**.

183   *See infra* **Table 15**. The difference between this and the baseline result is significant at the one-percent level. The verification rate for debt three to six years old was not significantly different than for baseline debt. Baseline debt was defined for the regression analysis as credit card debt that is less than 3 years old, acquired from the original creditor, with a face value less than $1000, and that had never been sent to a contingency collector.

184   *United States v. Kubrick*, 444 U.S. 111, 117 (1979).

may be seriously impaired by the loss of evidence, whether by death or disappearance of witnesses, fading memories, disappearance of documents, or otherwise."[185]

The protection that statutes of limitations provide to consumers is not automatic, however. In most states, the expiration of the statute of limitations on a debt does not extinguish the debt.[186] Instead, the running of the statute of limitations is an affirmative defense that consumers themselves must raise and prove before courts will dismiss actions to collect on their debts. As the Commission has noted, because 90% or more of consumers sued in these actions do not appear in court to defend, filing these actions creates a risk that consumers will be subject to a default judgment on a time-barred debt. To decrease this risk, the FTC has recommended that states change their laws to require collectors to prove that debts are not time-barred, rather than placing on consumers the burden of raising the defense of the running of the statute of limitations. The Commission further has recommended that states revise their laws to require that collectors plead the date of default and applicable statute of limitations in their complaints.[187]

1. LITIGATION AND THREATENED LITIGATION TO COLLECT ON TIME-BARRED DEBT

Both federal and state laws restrict the ability of debt buyers to file or threaten to file actions to recover on time-barred debts. It is well-established that it is a violation of the FDCPA for a debt collector (including a debt buyer) to file an action in court to collect on a time-barred debt.[188] It likewise is a clear violation of

---

185 *Id.*

186 In Mississippi and Wisconsin, the expiration of the statute of limitations extinguishes the debt. MISS. CODE ANN. § 15-1-3 (2012); WIS. STAT. ANN. § 893.05 (West 2012).

187 REPAIRING A BROKEN SYSTEM, *supra* note 3, at 30.

188 Bringing an action on time-barred debt has been held to be an unfair practice in violation of § 807, 15 U.S.C. § 1692e (2006). *See, e.g., Basile v. Blatt, Hasenmiller, Leibsker & Moore LLC,* 632 F. Supp. 2d 842, 845 (N.D. Ill. 2009) ("Courts have held that the filing of a time-barred lawsuit violates the FDCPA."); *Kimber v. Fed. Fin. Corp.,* 668 F. Supp. 1480, 1487 (M.D. Ala. 1987).

the FDCPA to threaten to file such an action.[189] States also have imposed new requirements designed to prevent or deter filing actions to recover on time-barred debts.[190]

Notwithstanding its clear illegality and the consensus among interested parties that collectors should not engage in it,[191] some consumer advocates contend and one recent study[192] concluded that debt buyers, in fact, do file or threaten to file actions to recover on time-barred debt.[193] The information the FTC received in response to its 6(b) orders did not permit the agency to assess how often debt buyers filed actions in court to recover on debts that were beyond the statute of limitations or the effect of such actions on consumers. In light of the concerns raised about such actions and recent changes in state law, however, the Commission concludes that further empirical work would be worthwhile to assess the prevalence of such actions and whether additional changes in law, procedures, or practice are needed to prevent or deter them.

2. DISCLOSURES REGARDING TIME-BARRED DEBT

Debt collectors, including debt buyers, may violate the law not only if they file an action to collect on time-barred debt, but also if they engage in deception in collecting on time-barred debt. When collectors attempt to recover on debts, in many circumstances, such efforts may convey or imply to consumers that the collectors could sue them if they do not pay. If the debts are time-barred, this message would be

---

189   Threatening to sue on time-barred debt has been held to violate various sections of the FDCPA: § 807, using false, deceptive, or misleading representations to collect a debt; § 807(2)(A), falsely representing the character, amount, or legal status of a debt; § 807(5), threatening to take an action that cannot legally be taken or that is not intended to be taken; and § 807(10), using a false representation or deceptive means to collect a debt. 15 U.S.C. § 1692e (2006); *see also, e.g.*, *Freyermuth v. Credit Bureau Servs., Inc.*, 248 F.3d 767, 771 (8th Cir. 2001) (holding by implication that the threat of litigation or actual litigation on a time-barred debt violates the FDCPA); *Walker v. Cash Flow Consultants, Inc.*, 200 F.R.D. 613, 616 (N.D. Ill. 2001) (finding that sending a collection letter that included a threat of litigation after the statute of limitations on the debt had expired would violate the FDCPA); *Beattie v. D.M. Collections, Inc.*, 754 F. Supp. 383, 393 (D. Del. 1991) ("[T]he threatening of a lawsuit which the debt collector knows or should know is unavailable or unwinnable by reason of a legal bar such as the statute of limitations is the kind of abusive practice the FDCPA was intended to eliminate."); *Kimber*, 668 F. Supp. at 1487 (finding that a debt collector violated the FDCPA when it filed a lawsuit on a time-barred debt without having first determined that the limitations period had actually been tolled).

190   North Carolina enacted a statute in 2009 that prohibits debt buyers, and those collecting on their behalf, from attempting to collect on time-barred debt and from receiving a default judgment or summary judgment without providing evidence establishing the date of last payment, which can be used to calculate the date on which the statute of limitations expires. N.C.G.S. § 58-70-115(4), 155(b)(7) (2012). Connecticut also altered its rules of civil procedure in 2010 to provide that a debt collection plaintiff bringing a small claims court action cannot be granted a default judgment without an affidavit stating "the basis upon which the plaintiff claims the statute of limitations has not expired." CONN. R. SUP. CT. § 24-24(b) (1)(B) (2012).

191   ACA CODE OF ETHICS, *supra* note 33, at 4; *see also* DBA INT'L, ETHICS RULES AND ETHICAL CONSIDERATIONS FOR DBA MEMBERS ER 5-102, *available at* http://www.dbainternational.org/what_is_dba/code_of_ethics.asp ("A Member shall not . . . [k]nowingly advance a claim or defense that is unwarranted under existing law, except that it may advance such claim or defense if it can be supported by good faith argument for an extension, modification, or reversal of existing law.").

192   A legal service provider in New York analyzed a sample of cases in its office and found that over 50% of cases for which sufficient information was available were based on debt for which the statute of limitations had expired. Letter from Robert A. Martin, Assoc. Dir., DC 37 Mun. Emps. Legal Servs., to the FTC (Feb. 11, 2010) (on file with the FTC) (supplementing the information described in WHERE'S THE PROOF?, *supra* note 124, at 9, 11).

193   *See, e.g.*, Nat'l Consumer Law Ctr. & Nat'l Ass'n of Consumer Advocates, *supra* note 120, at 3-4, 31-32; WHERE'S THE PROOF?, *supra* note 124, at 9, 11.

false or misleading, because the collectors in fact cannot legally file an action against them if they do not pay. Information about the consequences of not paying debts being collected appears to be important to consumers in deciding whether to pay debts and in what order to pay debts.[194]

Similar concerns arise when collectors request or accept partial payments on time-barred debts. When a collector makes such a request or accepts such a partial payment, in many circumstances, such efforts may convey or imply to consumers that they have only obligated themselves in the amount of the partial payment. For example, if a collector offers to accept a $50 payment on a $500 time-barred credit card debt, a consumer may believe that the $50 payment itself is the only consequence to him or her from making the payment. Nevertheless, under the laws of most states, a partial payment on a time-barred debt revives the entire balance of the debt for a new statute of limitations period.[195] This consequence likely would be important to consumers in deciding whether to make the payment.

In its 2010 Litigation Report, the FTC addressed whether debt collectors, including debt buyers, must make disclosures to prevent deception in collecting on time-barred debts. The report stated that "most consumers do not know or understand their legal rights with respect to the collection of time-barred debt," so attempts to collect on stale debt in many circumstances may create a misleading impression that the consumer could be sued, violating Section 5 of the FTC Act and Section 807 of the FDCPA.[196] To avoid creating such a misleading impression, the Commission stated that if a collector knows or should know that it is collecting on time-barred debt, then it generally must inform the consumer that "(1) the collector cannot sue to collect the debt and (2) providing a partial payment would revive the collector's ability to sue to collect the balance."[197] State and local governments similarly have started requiring that collectors must

---

194 A 2010 study examined whether consumers' responses to collection efforts are affected by the knowledge that a debt is time-barred. Goldsmith & Martin, *supra* note 40. The study concluded that "[t]hose participants who were told that the debt could not be enforced through court action chose different repayment options than participants who were not told about time-barred debt." *Id.* at 380. In the study, 34% of subjects said they would decline to pay a hypothetical debt when they were told the debt "cannot be enforced against you through court action because the enforcement period has run out." *Id.* at 377-80. Only 6% of subjects said they would decline to pay when they had not received the notice. *Id.* This difference was statistically significant. *Id.* at 378-79. The Goldsmith and Martin study therefore supports the notion that a debt's unenforceability is material to at least some consumers.

195 *See, e.g., Jenkins v. Gen. Collection Co.*, 538 F. Supp. 2d 1165, 1173 (D. Neb. 2008) ("Voluntary payment of any part of principal or interest tolls the statute of limitations and a new right of action accrues after each payment."); *United States v. Glens Falls Ins. Co.*, 546 F. Supp. 643, 645 (N.D.N.Y. 1982) ("[A]t common law, part payment of a debt starts the statute of limitations running anew in that part payment is tantamount to a voluntary acknowledgment of the existence of the debt, from which the law implies a new promise to pay the balance."); *Young v. Sorenson*, 121 Cal. Rptr. 236, 237 (Ct. App. 1975) ("[P]art payment of a debt or obligation is sufficient to extend the bar of the statute. The theory on which this is based is that the payment is an acknowledgment of the existence of the indebtedness which raises an implied promise to continue the obligation and to pay the balance."). Assuming in the example above that the state had a six-year statute of limitation period to file an action on credit card debts, then the $50 payment would revive the right to file an action for the $450 balance on the debt for six more years.

196 Repairing a Broken System, *supra* note 3, at 26.

197 *Id.* at 28.

disclose similar types of information to prevent deception and assist consumers in making better-informed decisions.[198]

The Commission recently brought an action against a debt buyer that allegedly collected on time-barred debt without disclosing to consumers that they could no longer be sued on the debt. The U.S. Department of Justice, on behalf of the FTC, filed a complaint against Asset Acceptance, LLC ("Asset") alleging that when Asset collects time-barred debt, "[m]any consumers do not know if the accounts that Asset is attempting to collect are beyond the statute of limitations. . . . When Asset contacts consumers to collect on a debt, many consumers believe they could experience serious negative consequences, including being sued, if they fail to pay the debt."[199] The complaint alleged that it was deceptive for Asset to fail to disclose to consumers that they could not be sued if they did not pay.[200] Asset agreed to a settlement under which it was required to disclose such information when it collects on debts that it knows or should know are time-barred.[201] Asset also agreed not to sue on time-barred debts for which it had made such disclosures as well as not to sell, transfer, or assign to another the right to sue on such debts. Following the Commission's action in *Asset Acceptance*, the Consumer Financial Protection Bureau recently entered into a settlement agreement with a bank collecting on its own debts that requires the bank to provide disclosures concerning the expiration of the bank's litigation rights when collecting debt that is barred by the applicable statute of limitations.[202]

---

198 In 2009, New York City enacted a law prohibiting debt collection agencies from collecting "a debt on which the statute of limitations for initiating legal action has expired unless such agency first provides the consumer such information about the consumer's legal rights as the commissioner prescribes by rule." N.Y.C. ADMIN. CODE § 20-493.2 (2012) (effective July 16, 2009). Following the FTC's 2009 report, the Attorney General of New Mexico also issued a rule in 2010 requiring debt collectors seeking to recover on debts they know or have reason to know are time-barred to disclose to consumers that they cannot be sued if they do not pay and that they will revive their debts under New Mexico law if they take certain actions. 21 N.M. Reg. 1191 (Dec. 15, 2010), *available at* http://www.nmcpr.state.nm.us/nmregister/xxi/xxi23/xxi23.pdf. In 2012, the Attorney General of Massachusetts further issued a regulation that requires collectors seeking to recover on debts they know or have reason to believe are time-barred to "disclose[] that the debt may be unenforceable through a lawsuit because the time for filing suit may have expired, and that the debtor is not required" to make any payment on the debt or take any other action that could waive the consumer's rights regarding the running of the statute of limitations. 940 MASS. CODE REGS. 7.07(24) (2012).

199 Complaint at ¶ 34, *United States v. Asset Acceptance, LLC*, No. 8:12-CV-182-T-27EAJ (M.D. Fla. Jan. 30, 2012), *available at* http://www.ftc.gov/opa/2012/01/asset.shtm. The Commission vote authorizing the staff to refer the complaint and consent decree to the Department of Justice was 3-1, with Commissioner J. Thomas Rosch voting no.

200 *Id.* at ¶¶ 81-82.

201 The *Asset*-required disclosure states that: (1) "The law limits how long [the consumer] can be sued on the debt," and (2) "Because of the age of [the consumer]'s debt, we will not sue [the consumer] for it." Consent Decree, *United States v. Asset Acceptance, LLC*, No. 8:12-cv-182-T-27EAJ (M.D. Fla. Jan. 31, 2012), *available at* http://www.ftc.gov/opa/2012/01/asset.shtm. FTC staff also recently closed an investigation of a debt buyer that had commenced disclosing clearly and prominently in collecting on time-barred debt that they could not sue consumers who did not pay. *See* Letter from Jessica Rich, Assoc. Dir., Div. of Fin. Practices, FTC, to Anthony E. DiResta, Esq., Counsel for RJM Acquisitions LLC (Aug. 27, 2012), *available at* http://www.ftc.gov/os/closings/staffclosing.shtm.

202 *In re Am. Express Centurion Bank, Salt Lake City, Utah*, FDIC-12-315b, FDIC-12-316k, 2012-CFPB-0002 (Oct. 1, 2012), at 6-7 (Joint Consent Order, Joint Order for Restitution, and Joint Order to Pay Civil Money Penalty), *available at* http://files.consumerfinance.gov/f/2012-CFPB-0002-American-Express-Centurion-Consent-Order.pdf.

The debt collection industry claims it is difficult to determine whether a debt is time-barred because different statutes of limitations could apply and there could be facts that tolled or restarted the statute of limitations.[203] The data the Commission received from debt buyers suggest that debt buyers usually are likely to know or be able to determine whether the debts on which they are collecting are beyond the statute of limitations. As discussed above, the information debt buyers receive as part of the process of bidding on debts and the information they receive when purchasing debts usually indicates the date of last payment or the charge-off dates for debts.[204] In most circumstances, this information should allow debt buyers to readily determine if debt is time-barred. Moreover, to the extent that there are questions about the date of last payment or charge-off information, it is unclear why debt buyers cannot seek this information from the original creditor or from a reseller of debt.

VIII. CONCLUSION

The FTC undertook this study to gain insight into debt buying and, in particular, to learn more about the information debt buyers obtain from sellers and use in the collection of debts. The study examined the information obtained and used at key stages in the debt buying and collection process – at the time of sale, when debt buyers initiate collection and send "validation notices" to consumers, when consumers dispute debts, and when debt buyers undertake to verify disputed debts.

This was the first major empirical study of debt buyers, and further analysis of certain issues clearly is needed. In particular, the study did not include data from any smaller debt buyers, firms that, in the FTC's experience, are frequently a source of consumer protection problems. The study also was not able to answer certain questions, such as why debt buyers did not disclose more information to consumers with validation notices, why they did not seek additional information post-sale, and why they did not verify nearly one-half of the disputed debts. The study also did not assess the litigation practices of debt buyers, a frequent source of consumer protection problems. Finally, the study did not directly examine the accuracy of the information debt buyers receive and use to collect debts. Consumers would benefit from future study and examination of these and other issues relating to debt buying.

---

203 ACA Int'l, Comments of ACA International in Response to the New Mexico Attorney General's Request for Comment Re: Revised Proposed Rules and Regulations Concerning Collection of Time-Barred Debts 4-5 (Feb. 27, 2009), *available at* http://www.acainternational.org/files.aspx?p=/images/13351/acanmformalcomments-time-barreddebt.pdf. A corollary of this argument is that if a debt collector incorrectly informs a consumer that a debt is time-barred, the debt collector could be liable under the FDCPA for making a material misrepresentation. *Id.*

204 Although there may be some circumstances in which debt buyers and other debt collectors may find it difficult to determine the relevant statute of limitations (*e.g.*, which state's law is applicable), in most circumstances the debt buyers in the study appear to have had the factual information necessary to determine whether the debts on which they were collecting were time-barred. Indeed, they would have had to make these determinations about debts to avoid violating the FDCPA through suing or threatening to sue on time-barred debts.

Since the Commission launched its study of debt buyers, it has continued to receive a high level of complaints regarding debt collectors, more than for any other industry. Many of these complaints reported that debt collectors were attempting to collect debts the consumer did not owe, or, if they did owe debts, for amounts that were greater than what was actually owed. Thus, the sufficiency and accuracy of the information used in the collection of debts remains a significant consumer protection concern. The Commission hopes that this debt buyer study will contribute to a greater understanding of debt buying, enhance ongoing reform efforts in the debt buyer industry, and prompt further study of the industry and its practices.

TABLES

Table 1:   Debt Buyers in FTC Study[1]

Company Name	Total Consumer Debt Bought in 2008 (by face value, in billions)	Consumer Debt Bought Directly from Credit Card Issuers in 2008 (by face value, in billions)
Sherman Financial Group LLC, New York, NY	$16.00	$15.48
Encore Capital Group Inc., San Diego, CA	$6.56	$4.22
eCAST Settlement Corp., New York, NY	$5.86	$3.47
NCO Portfolio Management, Inc., Horsham, PA	$5.40	$1.60 (est.)
Arrow Financial Services LLC, Niles, IL	$5.07	$4.60
Portfolio Recovery Associates, LLC, Norfolk, VA	$4.58	$3.89 (est.)
Unifund Corp., Cincinnati, OH	$4.30	$3.60
B-Line, LLC, Seattle, WA	$3.76	$3.39
Asta Funding, Inc., Englewood Cliffs, NJ	$3.49	$3.14 (est.)
TOTAL	**$55.02**	**$43.39**

[1] *Credit Card Debt Sales in 2008*, 921 NILSON REP. 10 (Mar. 2009) [hereinafter NILSON REPORT], including all estimated figures. Although *The Nilson Report's* methodology in obtaining these data is unknown, the data are widely cited within the collections industry, and even if imprecise or generated by a proprietary methodology, are likely to reflect the relative positions of firms and year-to-year trends. *See* U.S. GOV'T ACCOUNTABILITY OFFICE, CREDIT CARDS: FAIR DEBT COLLECTION PRACTICES ACT COULD BETTER REFLECT THE EVOLVING DEBT COLLECTION MARKETPLACE AND USE OF TECHNOLOGY (2009), http://www.gao.gov/new.items/d09748.pdf (citing NILSON REPORT, but noting that NILSON REPORT officials declined the GAO's request to discuss the methodology employed in obtaining data); KAULKIN GINSBERG, GLOBAL DEBT BUYING REPORT: EXPERTS ANALYZE THE WORLDWIDE DEBT BUYING MARKET 17-18 (2006) (explaining NILSON REPORT'S reasons for declining to disclose methodology). Data from 2008 were used to determine recipients of the Commission's order, as those were the most recent available data at the time the study was designed.

Table 2:   Basic Characteristics of Submitted Portfolios

Account status at time of purchase	Portfolios		Accounts		Face Values (a)			Acquisition Expenditures (b)		
	#	%	#	%	$	%	Avg. FV of accounts	$	%	per $ of Face Value
Charge-off	3,087	61%	77,675,862	87%	$104,733,044,243	73%	$1,348	$5,014,641,267	78%	$0.04788
Bankruptcy	1,966	39%	11,357,757	13%	$38,194,615,739	27%	$3,363	$1,426,349,243	22%	$0.03734
Total	5,053	100%	89,033,619	100%	$142,927,659,982	100%	$1,605	$6,440,990,510	100%	$0.04506

Table Notes:

(a) Aggregate face values were computed by multiplying the average face value of accounts in each portfolio (as requested at specification II.A.3.g) by the number of accounts in each portfolio (as requested at specification II.A.3.c), and then summing across all relevant portfolios. Average face value figures were calculated by dividing the relevant aggregate face value by the relevant aggregate number of accounts.

(b) Specification II.A.3.e requested the amount paid for each portfolio. Acquisition expenditures per dollar of face value figures were calculated by summing the amount paid for each portfolio across all relevant portfolios and then dividing by the relevant total face value as described in (a), above.

Table 3: <u>**Charged-Off Credit Card Accounts Debt Buyers Purchased Directly from Creditors**</u>

	Year						
	2005	2006	2007	2008	2009	2010	2011
Face Value of Charged-off Credit Card Debt Purchased Directly From Credit Card Issuers, in $ Billion	$66.44	$52.59	$68.23	$55.53	$44.20	$40.32	$51.78
Above, as a Percentage of the Face Value of All Debt Purchased by Debt Buyers	75%	89%	75%	77%	74%	75%	81%

Source: *The Nilson Report*, Issue Nos. 857, 880, 901, 921, 946, 969, and 992. *See n.1, Table 1, supra*, regarding *Nilson Report* data.

Table 4:   Characteristics of Portfolios Submitted by Nine Debt Buyers

Type of Debt Accounts Within Charge-off Portfolios (a)	Portfolios		Accounts		Face Values (m)		Acquisition Expenditures (n)	
	#	% of All Charge-off Portfolios	#	% of All Charge-off Accounts	% of All Charge-off Portfolios	Avg. Face Value of Accounts	% of Charge-off Portfolios	Per $ of Face Value
Credit Card (b)	1918	62%	35,220,694	45%	65%	$1,943	71%	$0.05224
Medical (c)	530	17%	21,500,329	28%	7%	$345	3%	$0.01909
Consumer Loans (d)	161	5%	1,014,011	1%	4%	$3,785	2%	$0.03219
Utilities	73	2%	1,483,133	2%	1%	$480	0%	$0.01718
Telecomm	68	2%	11,299,647	15%	5%	$438	3%	$0.02983
Mixed (e)	66	2%	2,067,028	3%	6%	$3,026	3%	$0.02595
Auto Loans (f)	59	2%	1,084,058	1%	7%	$6,489	2%	$0.01560
Other (g)	57	2%	2,832,530	4%	2%	$898	2%	$0.03229
"Credit cards & Lines of Credit"(h)	54	2%	276,779	0%	2%	$7,229	3%	$0.06598
Student Loans	52	2%	416,974	1%	0%	$735	0%	$0.03484
Mortgages(i)	35	1%	20,683	0%	1%	$48,669	10%	$0.50442
Overdrafts	8	0%	439,651	1%	0%	$447	0%	$0.05017
Not Stated	4	0%	155	0%	0%	n/a	0%	$0.00094
Bad Checks	2	0%	20,190	0%	0%	$156	0%	$0.01944
Sub-total (j)	3087	100%	77,675,862	100%	100%	$1,348	100%	$0.04788
Type of Bankruptcy Filing Within Bankruptcy Portfolios	#	% of All BK Portfolios	#	% of All BK Accounts	% of All BK Portfolios	Avg. Face Value of Accounts	% of BK Portfolios	Per $ of Face Value
Bankruptcy Portfolios:(k)								
Chp. 13 Bankruptcy (l)	1690	86%	7,977,364	70%	61%	$2,931	99%	$0.06067
Chp. 7 Bankruptcy	276	14%	3,380,393	30%	39%	$4,382	1%	$0.00052
Sub-total	1966	100%	11,357,757	100%	100%	$3,363	100%	$0.03734
Total of All Portfolios	5053		89,033,619			$1,605		$0.04506

Table Notes:

(a) Firms freely designated account descriptors.

(b) "Credit Card" includes general purpose credit cards (often specifically designated as "Visa," "MasterCard," etc.) as well as accounts designated "private label credit card," "subprime credit card," "consumer credit card," and "business credit card." Although we collectively treat these as "credit cards," the distinctions among sub-types may be important to firms. See, for example, Portfolio Recovery Associates' 10-K report for the year ended December 31, 2009, at p. 7, where "major credit cards" are distinguished from "private label credit cards" when listing "Life to Date Purchased Face Value of Defaulted Consumer Receivables."

(c) "Medical" includes accounts designated by some firms as "healthcare." A small percentage of these portfolios were comprised of accounts with very high average face values (*e.g.*, five and even six figure amounts) that suggest large hospital bills. The vast majority of the portfolios, however, were comprised of accounts that had low and mid three figure balances, as reflected by the average face value of accounts calculated for all submitted medical portfolios.

(d) "Consumer Loans" also includes accounts designated as "installment loans," "personal loans," and "unsecured consumer loans."

(e) "Mixed" includes firms' own use of the descriptor "mixed" as well as instances where firms used multiple account descriptors within portfolios (*e.g.*, "credit card, consumer loans, auto," or "credit card, auto, consumer loan, installment loan, telecom," etc.) and we assigned the term "mixed." "Credit cards" were expressly mentioned in "mixed" portfolios more often than any other descriptors (58 portfolios) and "auto" was the second most frequently used descriptor (25 portfolios). Accordingly, the true percentages of all submitted accounts that fell into the categories "credit card" and "auto" exceed the percentages attributed to these categories in the table.

(Table continued on next page.)

Table 4:   Characteristics of Portfolios Submitted by Nine Debt Buyers (continued)

Table Notes (continued):

(f) "Auto Loans" may include loans that are secured by vehicles as well as unsecured loans (*i.e.*, auto loan deficiencies) which result when the value of repossessed autos fall short of the outstanding loan amounts.

(g) This includes instances where firms self-reported "other" or "misc." as the type of debt, as well as some express but infrequently used debt account descriptors, such as "debt consolidation service."

(h) Several firms used the express descriptor "credit cards and lines of credit," even though they also report "credit cards." No firms reported portfolios comprised solely of "lines of credit." Because of this, we have opted to break-out "credit cards & lines of credit" as a separate category. While these portfolios could have been placed into the "mixed" category, that would have obscured the fact that "credit cards & lines of credit" portfolios had average face values ($7,229) that were more than twice the average face values of other "mixed" portfolios ($3,026).

(i) The average expenditure per dollar of face value for mortgage accounts is sensitive to the presence of a small number of mortgage portfolios for which the average acquisition expenditures per dollar of face value was in excess of 75 cents on the dollar; some of these portfolios were expressly linked to contracts for the purchase of performing mortgage loans. In contrast, a significant number of mortgage portfolios had average acquisition expenditures per dollar of face value that were below one cent on the dollar; some of these portfolios were expressly linked to contracts which indicated that the portfolios pertained to properties that had already been foreclosed on and/or for which the consumer had declared bankruptcy. The median acquisition expenditure per dollar of face value for all mortgage portfolios was $0.10000, or ten cents on the dollar.

(j) Cumulative rounding errors may prevent percentage figures from summing to 100%.

(k) Five of the seven firms who reported purchases of bankruptcy portfolios also revealed the type of debt within the portfolios; 84% of their bankruptcy portfolios were comprised of credit card debt. These five firms purchased 72% of the 1,966 self-reported bankruptcy portfolios. Accordingly, we estimate that at least 60% of all bankruptcy portfolios are comprised of credit card debt (84% of 72% is 60%).

(l) Three firms expressly indicated the Bankruptcy Chapter pertaining to their self-reported bankruptcy portfolios. Three other firms indicated in their narrative reports that virtually all of their purchases of bankruptcy portfolios pertained to Chapter 13 filings. One firm used "Paying Bankruptcy" as a descriptor, and we have assumed that to indicate a Chapter 13 bankruptcy.

(m) To conserve space horizontally, the aggregate face values for each type of debt account have been omitted. Aggregate face values were computed by multiplying the average face value of accounts in each portfolio (as requested at specification II.A.3.g) by the number of accounts in each portfolio (as requested at specification II.A.3.c), and then summing across all portfolios of the same type. Average face value figures were calculated by dividing the relevant aggregate face value by the relevant aggregate number of accounts.

(n) To conserve space horizontally, the aggregate acquisition expenses for each type of debt account have been omitted. Specification II.A.3.e requested the amount paid for each portfolio. Acquisition expenditures per dollar of face value figures were calculated by summing the amount paid for each portfolio across all portfolios of the same type and then dividing by the relevant total face value as described in (m), above.

Table 5: **The 10 Largest Direct Purchasers of Consumer Debt from Credit Card Issuers, by Year, 2005 to 2011**

Firm Name	Firm Rank for Direct Purchases of Credit Card Debt (by Face Value), as Given by *The Nilson Report*, by Year						
	2005	2006	2007	2008	2009	2010	2011*
Sherman Financial	1	1	1	1	1	2	1
Arrow Financial	10	6	6	2	n/a	n/a	n/a
Encore Capital	5	10	5	3	2	1	2
Portfolio Recovery	7	2	2	4	4	4	3
Unifund	4	3	4	5	5	5	8
eCast	8	5	9	6	n/a	n/a	9
B-Line	3	n/a	8	7	n/a	10	10
Asta Funding	6	4	3	8	10	n/a	n/a
Asset Acceptance	n/a	7	7	9	6	6	5
Collect America/Square Two Financial	9	8	10	10	7	3	4
NCO Portfolio Mgmt.	2	n/a	n/a	n/a	9	n/a	n/a
Zenith Acquisitions	n/a	n/a	n/a	n/a	3	9	n/a
Ophrys	n/a	n/a	n/a	n/a	8	7	6
Fourscore	n/a	9	n/a	n/a	n/a	8	7

Source: Data for this table were drawn from *The Nilson Report*, Issue Nos. 857, 880, 901, 921, 946, 969, and 992. A rank "n/a" in any given year may mean either that the firm was not in the top 10 firms, or that they were not ranked at all. Some unranked firms may have exited the industry, or not yet entered the industry.

Table 6:   Sample Characteristics of Debts Purchased by Six Debt Buyers

Debt Characteristics	Debt Acquired from:		
	Original Creditor	Debt Buyer	All Sellers
Average Price Per Dollar of Debt	$0.043	$0.029	$0.040
Debt Age:			
0 to 3 years	75.2%	37.9%	68.2%
3+ to 6 years	16.3%	32.1%	19.3%
6+ to 15 years	7.5%	27.5%	11.3%
15+ years	0.4%	2.6%	0.8%
Not Reported	0.6%	0.0%	0.5%
Debt Face Value:			
0 to 1 thousand dollars	72.5%	67.4%	71.5%
1+ to 5 thousand dollars	20.0%	25.2%	21.0%
5+ to 20 thousand dollars	7.0%	6.7%	6.9%
20+ thousand dollars	0.5%	0.7%	0.5%
Account Type:			
Auto Loans	1.4%	18.5%	4.6%
Consumer Loans	1.5%	0.1%	1.2%
Credit Cards	36.4%	49.0%	38.8%
Medical	33.4%	0.0%	27.1%
Mortgages	0.0%	0.0%	0.0%
Overdraft	0.2%	0.0%	0.2%
Telecommunications	16.3%	9.1%	15.0%
Utility	2.2%	0.0%	1.7%
Other	8.7%	23.4%	11.5%
Previously Sent to Contingency Collector	47.8%	57.5%	49.6%
Previously Sent to Contingency Collector: Not Reported	47.1%	31.7%	44.2%
Not Acquired from Original Creditor	0.0%	100.0%	18.8%
# of Portfolio Observations	3,036	363	3,399
# of Accounts	61,534,019	14,281,636	75,815,655

Notes: All percentages are of purchased debt accounts. The distributions of debt age and face value were calculated assuming a gamma distribution characterized by the portfolio average and standard deviation of these variables.

Table 7: Regression Model of Purchase Price Per Dollar of Debt

Variables	Coeff.	Std. Error	
Baseline Price Per Dollar	**$0.079**	**$0.008**	***
Debt Age:			
3+ to 6 years	-$0.048	$0.005	***
6+ to 15 years	-$0.057	$0.006	***
15+ years	-$0.092	$0.027	***
Not Reported	$0.012	$0.037	
Debt Face Value:			
1+ to 5 thousand dollars	$0.002	$0.015	
5+ to 20 thousand dollars	-$0.023	$0.024	
20+ thousand dollars	-$0.066	$0.183	
Account Type:			
Auto Loans	-$0.011	$0.007	
Consumer Loans	-$0.011	$0.005	**
Medical	-$0.030	$0.006	***
Mortgages	$0.479	$0.169	***
Overdraft	-$0.011	$0.008	
Telecommunications	-$0.017	$0.006	***
Utility	-$0.036	$0.008	***
Other	-$0.030	$0.005	***
Previously Sent to Contingency Collector	-$0.014	$0.003	***
Previously Sent to Contingency Collector: Not Reported	-$0.016	$0.004	***
Not Acquired from Original Creditor	$0.004	$0.004	
R^2		0.65	
# of Portfolio Observations		3,399	
Total Face Value of All Accounts		$114,051,119,500	

Notes: While the model is estimated using portfolio aggregates, it is equivalent to a model estimated using account-level data. Model includes debt buyer fixed effects for the six firms included in the estimation sample. The baseline corresponds to a credit card debt that is less than 3 years old, acquired from the original creditor, with a face value less than one thousand dollars, and that had never been sent to a contingency collector. The predicted price per dollar is averaged across all debt buyers. Robust standard errors are reported. Statistical significance is denoted by "***" when significant at the 1% level, "**" when significant at the 5% level, and "*" when significant at the 10% level.

Table 8: Data File Information Obtained at Time of Sale[1]

Type of Information	Percentage of Accounts for Which Debt Buyers Obtained the Specified Information at Time of Purchase (5,087,032 Accounts)[2]	Percentage of Portfolios for Which Debt Buyers Obtained the Specified Information for Any Account at the Time of Purchase (511 Portfolios)[2]	Percentage of Accounts for Which Debt Buyers Obtained the Specified Information at Time of Purchase for Selected Types of Debt[3]					
			Credit Cards (3,973,695 Accounts)	Consumer Loans (51,036 Accounts)	Medical (206,900 Accounts)	Utility (24,895 Accounts)	CH 7 Bankruptcy (220,801 Accounts)	CH 13 Bankruptcy (28,846 Accounts)
Account Information								
Original Account Number	100%	100%	100%	100%	100%	100%	100%	100%
Original Creditor Name	46%	52%	43%	43%	0%	0%	79%	2%
Account Open Date	97%	93%	99%	96%	65%	0%	100%	100%
Type of Debt	62%	36%	71%	65%	18%	100%	0%	0%
Credit Limit	10%	17%	7%	0%	0%	0%	53%	0%
Interest Rate	30%	23%	30%	40%	0%	0%	46%	0%
Debtor Information								
Name	100%	100%	100%	100%	97%	100%	100%	100%
Social Security Number	98%	98%	98%	100%	96%	82%	100%	100%
Street Address	99%	97%	100%	100%	97%	0%	100%	100%
Home Telephone Number	70%	91%	68%	88%	66%	0%	100%	88%
Work Telephone Number	47%	85%	43%	73%	14%	0%	96%	72%
Mobile Telephone Number	15%	33%	11%	11%	0%	0%	79%	2%
Birth Date	65%	65%	64%	54%	66%	0%	98%	2%
Credit Score	<1%	1%	<1%	0%	0%	0%	0%	0%
Balance								
Current Balance	100%	100%	100%	100%	97%	100%	100%	100%
Balance Breakdown								
Balance at Charge-Off	72%	70%	74%	73%	48%	0%	99%	97%
Principal Amount[4]	11%	12%	9%	30%	32%	0%	0%	0%
Principal Amount or Charge-Off Balance	82%	78%	82%	75%	66%	0%	99%	97%
Finance Charges and Fees[5]	37%	39%	43%	1%	0%	0%	0%	0%

(Table continued on next page.)

Table 8:   Data File Information Obtained at Time of Sale (continued)

Type of Information	Percentage of Accounts for Which Debt Buyers Obtained the Specified Information at Time of Purchase (5,087,032 Accounts)[2]	Percentage of Portfolios for Which Debt Buyers Obtained the Specified Information for Any Account at the Time of Purchase (511 Portfolios)[2]	Percentage of Accounts for Which Debt Buyers Obtained the Specified Information at Time of Purchase for Selected Types of Debt[3]					
			Credit Cards (3,973,695 Accounts)	Consumer Loans (51,036 Accounts)	Medical (206,900 Accounts)	Utility (24,895 Accounts)	CH 7 Bankruptcy (220,801 Accounts)	CH 13 Bankruptcy (28,846 Accounts)
Key Dates[6]								
Date of Last Payment	90%	92%	93%	70%	49%	0%	98%	96%
Date of Charge-Off	83%	91%	89%	100%	14%	0%	74%	99%
Date of First Default	35%	28%	41%	25%	0%	0%	0%	7%

Table Notes

[1] This table is based on responses to specification II.D.1 by six going-concern debt buyers not specialized to bankruptcy recoveries. Four firms submitted data on all portfolios purchased in the relevant time period (March through August of 2009). Two firms did not hold the requested data in spreadsheet form and were permitted to provide a small sample from portfolios purchased in the relevant period in order to reduce their costs of compliance.

[2] These figures are based on information from all responses received to specification II.D.1.

[3] These figures are based on accounts for which we were able to identify the type of debt. Type of debt was identified either by matching the portfolio, through its portfolio identification number, to data provided in response to specification II.A.3 (limited to the overlap period of March through June of 2009) or through other information that accompanied the portfolio, for example, sometimes the portfolio name identified the type of debt, sometimes data within the portfolio identified the type of debt, and sometimes other exhibits or correspondence from the debt buyer identified the type of debt. The type of debt was identified for 91% of the accounts and 82% of the portfolios submitted. Although data responsive to II.D.1 did not always include information on the type of debt, debt buyers would likely obtain this information in the process of purchasing debt portfolios.

[4] "Principal Amount" may be less relevant for revolving forms of debt, such as credit cards, than it is for closed-end loans.

[5] "Finance Charges and Fees" reflects an aggregation of the variety of fees and finance charges found in the data fields. Some of these charges were further distinguished by specific dates or events (e.g., at or since delinquency, at or since charge-off, etc.). Reporting styles varied greatly across portfolios.

[6] The date of last payment, charge-off or first default can be used to determine when a debt falls outside of the statute of limitations.

Table 9: Documents Obtained at Time of Sale

Type of Document	Percentage of Accounts for Which Debt Buyers Received the Specified Document at Time of Purchase (3,862,018Accounts)	Percentage of Portfolios for Which Debt Buyers Received the Specified Document for Any Account at the Time of Purchase (333 Portfolios)[2]
Any Document	12%	13%
Account Statements	6%	9%
Terms and Conditions	6%	3%
Account Applications	< 1%	3%

Table Notes

[1] This table is based on responses to specification II.D.1 by six going-concern debt buyers not specialized to bankruptcy recoveries. Three debt buyers submitted information on all portfolios purchased in the relevant time period (March through August of 2009). The other three debt buyers did not have the information readily available, and because of the likely burden of compiling it, were permitted to provide the information for a small sample of the portfolios purchased during the period. About 52% of the accounts in the portfolios for which the FTC received information were submitted by one buyer, and about 87% were submitted by two buyers. If data from the debt buyers that submitted only samples of their portfolios are weighted by the total number of accounts and portfolios purchased in this time period, the estimated percentage of accounts for which any document was received at the time of purchase decreases to 6% and the estimated number of portfolios in which any document was received increases to 20%.

[2] About 1.5% of portfolios came with more than one type of document.

Table 10: Breakdown of Debt Buyer Actions After Purchase

| | Debt Acquired from: | | |
	Original Creditor	Debt Buyer	All Sellers
Attempted to Collect:			
Internally Only	24.3%	37.3%	26.8%
w/ Contingency Collectors Only	32.0%	17.7%	29.2%
Internally & w/ Contingency Collectors	31.6%	33.0%	31.9%
All	*87.9%*	*88.0%*	*87.9%*
No Attempt to Collect:			
Subsequently Not Sold	7.3%	9.1%	7.6%
Subsequently Sold	4.9%	2.9%	4.5%
All	*12.1%*	*12.0%*	*12.1%*
# of Portfolio Observations	1,984	271	2,255
# of Accounts	28,076,421	6,853,756	34,930,177

Table 11: Regression Models of the Probability that Debt Buyers Attempt Different Collection Methods

Variables	Attempted to Collect Internally			Sent to Contingency Collector		
	Coeff.	Std. Error		Coeff.	Std. Error	
Baseline Probability of Collection Attempt	**64.10%**	**5.92%**	***	**77.96%**	**7.17%**	***
Debt Age:						
3+ to 6 years	16.14%	5.70%	***	-6.32%	7.59%	
6+ to 15 years	20.80%	6.17%	***	17.22%	8.57%	**
15+ years	36.71%	44.68%		-55.77%	31.66%	*
Not Reported	-8.09%	3.21%	**	-25.22%	16.61%	
Debt Face Value:						
1+ to 5 thousand dollars	-12.76%	11.79%		-23.57%	11.35%	**
5+ to 20 thousand dollars	1.87%	13.05%		-10.62%	15.22%	
20+ thousand dollars	-90.08%	73.90%		-51.36%	54.03%	
Account Type:						
Auto Loans	-36.85%	13.14%	***	-9.62%	5.71%	*
Consumer Loans	5.72%	4.97%		5.85%	4.00%	
Medical	-7.67%	5.32%		-32.18%	6.67%	***
Mortgages	149.65%	53.90%	***	-20.98%	45.85%	
Overdraft	-0.24%	4.89%		-7.67%	9.49%	
Telecommunications	24.22%	6.77%	***	-10.82%	4.51%	**
Utility	8.40%	3.81%	**	-23.76%	3.76%	***
Other	-9.04%	3.91%	**	-47.35%	10.90%	***
Previously Sent to Contingency Collector	-7.70%	3.66%	**	4.65%	2.60%	*
Previously Sent to Contingency Collector: Not Reported	-6.29%	4.63%		9.41%	3.18%	***
Not Acquired from Original Creditor	-13.22%	5.04%	***	2.80%	3.96%	
R^2		0.77			0.75	
# of Portfolio Observations		2,514			2,722	
# of Accounts		39,733,260			45,869,466	

Notes: Results are reported for separate regressions. Collection attempt outcomes are not mutually exclusive. While the models are estimated using portfolio aggregates, they are equivalent to linear probability models estimated using account-level data. Therefore, predicted probabilities are not constrained between 0 and 100 percent. Models include debt buyer fixed effects for the five firms included in the estimation sample. The baseline corresponds to a credit card debt that is less than 3 years old, acquired from the original creditor, with a face value less than one thousand dollars, and that had never been sent to a contingency collector. The predicted probability is averaged across all debt buyers. Robust standard errors are reported. Statistical significance is denoted by "***" when significant at the 1% level, "**" when significant at the 5% level, and "*" when significant at the 10% level.

Table 12: <u>Regression Model of the Probability of Accounts Receiving Internal Collection Attempts Being Subsequently Disputed</u>

Variables	Coeff.	Std. Error	
Baseline Probability of Dispute	**0.03%**	**2.51%**	
<u>Debt Age:</u>			
3+ to 6 years	0.68%	1.17%	
6+ years	-0.73%	1.25%	
Not Reported	4.28%	8.38%	
<u>Debt Face Value:</u>			
1+ to 5 thousand dollars	1.84%	3.26%	
5+ to 20 thousand dollars	1.23%	4.10%	
20+ thousand dollars	-0.35%	10.92%	
<u>Account Type:</u>			
Auto Loans	0.05%	1.81%	
Consumer Loans	-2.69%	1.32%	**
Medical	-0.27%	0.87%	
Mortgages	-10.04%	9.34%	
Overdraft	0.68%	4.97%	
Telecommunications	0.72%	0.76%	
Utility	-0.02%	0.64%	
Other	1.15%	1.12%	
Previously Sent to Contingency Collector	1.92%	0.48%	***
Previously Sent to Contingency Collector: Not Reported	1.09%	0.85%	
Not Acquired from Original Creditor	-1.34%	0.98%	
R^2		0.36	
# of Portfolio Observations		2,114	
# of Accounts		16,445,501	

Notes: While the model is estimated using portfolio aggregates, it is equivalent to a linear probability model estimated using account-level data. Therefore, predicted probabilities are not constrained between 0 and 100 percent. The model includes debt buyer fixed effects for the four firms included in the estimation sample. The baseline corresponds to a credit card debt that is less than 3 years old, acquired from the original creditor, with a face value less than one thousand dollars, and that had never been sent to a contingency collector. The predicted probability is averaged across all debt buyers. Because of the extremely small number of accounts with ages above fifteen years that received a collection attempt by debt buyers, the "15+ years" category was collapsed into the "6+ to 15 years" category for the estimation of the dispute rate and verification rate models. All regressors are imputed based on portfolio-level aggregates and the corresponding standard errors are bootstrapped accordingly. Statistical significance is denoted by "***" when significant at the 1% level, "**" when significant at the 5% level, and "*" when significant at the 10% level.

Table 13:   Documents Obtained After Sale[1]

Type of Document	Percentage of Accounts for Which Debt Buyers Obtained the Specified Document After Purchase (1,477,720 Accounts)	Percentage of Portfolios for Which Debt Buyers Obtained the Specified Document for Any Account After Purchase (202 Portfolios)
Account Statements	6%[2]	97%[3]
Terms and Conditions	8%[4]	8%
Account Applications	6%[5]	57%
Payment History Documents	< 1%	11%
Affidavits	<1%	28%
All Other Types of Documents, Combined	<1%	24%

Table Notes

[1] This table is based on responses to specification II.D.2 submitted by five of the six going-concern debt buyers not specialized to bankruptcy recoveries. (The sixth firm did not submit a response because it held the requested information in a manner that would have required a costly manual review even if sampling had been used.) None of these five firms submitted information for all portfolios purchased during the relevant time period (March through August of 2009). Two firms submitted information for large subsets of the portfolios they purchased during the period. No sampling method was identified in their responses, possibly suggesting the submitted information represented all of the portfolios for which any documents were obtained post-purchase. Combined, these two firms submitted the information on 85% of the accounts and 86% of the portfolios used in this analysis. The remaining three firms provided small random samples drawn from portfolios purchased during the period.

[2] This figure is based on information provided by three firms. These three firms each provided the number of accounts for which particular types of documents were obtained. Their responses comprised 85% of the accounts and 90% of the portfolios for which information was submitted. The other two firms submitted information on the number of documents obtained, but not on the number of accounts for which they obtained documents. However, one or both of these firms are included in the tabulations for some of the other types of documents, as explained below.

[3] This figure is based on information provided by four firms. Together, these four firms submitted the information on 94% of the portfolios used in this analysis. The fifth firm reported the aggregate number of account statements obtained but not indicate how these documents corresponded with particular portfolios.

[4] This figure is based on information from four firms. In addition to the three firms noted in table note 2, above, one of the other two firms reported that they did not obtain any terms and conditions documents, implying that the number of accounts for which terms and conditions documents were obtained was zero.

[5] This figure is based on information from all five firms. In addition to the three firms noted in table note 2, above, the other two firms reported that they did not obtain any application documents, implying that the number of accounts for which application documents were obtained was zero.

Table 14: Breakdown of Debt Buyer Actions After Receiving Dispute

	Debt Acquired from:		
	Original Creditor	Debt Buyer	All Sellers
Verified Debt:			
Subsequently Not Sold	53.3%	32.4%	48.8%
Subsequently Sold	2.5%	3.5%	2.5%
All	*55.7%*	*35.9%*	*51.3%*
Did Not Verify Debt:			
Subsequently Not Sold	43.9%	63.8%	48.3%
Subsequently Sold	0.4%	0.3%	0.4%
All	*44.3%*	*64.1%*	*48.7%*
# of Portfolio Observations	1,686	167	1,853
# of Accounts	553,587	159,721	713,308

Notes: The proportion of verified/non-verified debts that are subsequently sold is imputed based on the two firms that reported this information.

Table 15: **Regression Model of the Probability of Disputed Accounts Being Verified**

Variables	Coeff.	Std. Error	
Baseline Probability of Verification	**58.40%**	**2.89%**	***
Debt Age:			
3+ to 6 years	0.60%	3.85%	
6+ years	-22.33%	3.84%	***
Not Reported	11.43%	15.32%	
Debt Face Value:			
1+ to 5 thousand dollars	14.47%	37.67%	
5+ thousand dollars	-9.65%	18.11%	
Account Type:			
Auto Loans	0.18%	8.15%	
Consumer Loans	1.68%	3.12%	
Medical	-14.23%	4.00%	***
Mortgages	-21.93%	23.25%	
Overdraft	-4.14%	10.41%	
Telecommunications	-15.67%	3.34%	***
Utility	-8.55%	2.08%	***
Other	3.90%	2.73%	
Previously Sent to Contingency Collector	4.26%	1.83%	**
Previously Sent to Contingency Collector: Not Reported	6.42%	2.27%	***
Not Acquired from Original Creditor	-7.06%	3.74%	*
R^2		0.82	
# of Portfolio Observations		1,692	
# of Accounts		527,319	

Notes: While the model is estimated using portfolio aggregates, it is equivalent to a linear probability model estimated using account-level data. Therefore, predicted probabilities are not constrained between 0 and 100 percent. Model includes debt buyer fixed effects for the three firms included in the estimation sample. The baseline corresponds to a credit card debt that is less than 3 years old, acquired from the original creditor, with a face value less than one thousand dollars, and that had never been sent to a contingency collector. The predicted probability is averaged across all debt buyers. Because of the extremely small number of accounts with face values above twenty thousand dollars that received a collection attempt by debt buyers and that were subsequently disputed, the "20+ thousand dollar" category was collapsed into the "5-20 thousand dollar" category for the estimation of the verification rate model. All regressors are imputed based on portfolio-level aggregates and the corresponding standard errors are bootstrapped accordingly. Statistical significance is denoted by "***" when significant at the 1% level, "**" when significant at the 5% level, and "*" when significant at the 10% level.

TECHNICAL APPENDIX A:
6(B) ORDERS SENT TO DEBT BUYERS

Technical Appendix A: 6(b) Orders Sent to Debt Buyers

To better understand what information the debt buyers obtained from sellers prior to purchasing debt portfolios, the orders required the debt buyers to provide the following for portfolios they purchased or bid on: (1) advertising and other marketing materials, (2) information and documentation relating to the portfolio that the debt buyer obtained before deciding whether to bid on the portfolio, and (3) a description of the process through which they learned of portfolios being offered for sale and the process they used to evaluate a portfolio before determining whether to bid on it.[1]

The Commission also obtained data about debt portfolios that the debt buyers purchased during a three-year period between July 2006 and June 2009, including: (1) the number and types of consumer debt accounts in each portfolio purchased; (2) the average age and face value of the accounts; and (3) the amount the debt buyer paid for the portfolio.[2]

The orders further asked the debt buyers to describe the information and documents about portfolios they obtain from sellers at the time of purchase, including whether, and in what ways, this information varies depending on the type of debt in the portfolio (*e.g.*, credit card, auto loan, or medical debt).[3] The debt buyers also produced copies of a number of the contracts that they entered into with sellers to purchase debt portfolios.[4] In addition, for a sample of portfolios purchased between March 2009 and August 2009, the Commission obtained the information that

---

[1] *See infra* Exhibit 1, Specification II.B.2, II.B.3, and II.B.4.

[2] *Id.* at Specification II.A.3.

[3] *Id.* at Specification II.D.1.

[4] *Id.* at Specification II.C.1 and II.C.2.

the debt buyer obtained from the seller at the time of purchase.[5]

The orders also required the debt buyers to describe the terms and conditions under which they were permitted to obtain additional information from the seller about accounts in a portfolio after the time of purchase. The debt buyers were required to provide the additional information they obtained after the time of purchase for a sample of portfolios purchased during the period March 2009 through August 2009.[6]

The Commission also obtained data about how debt buyers handled accounts after they were purchased. For example, the debt buyers were required to state how many accounts they attempted to collect using in-house collectors, how many they sent to third-party collection agencies, and how many they resold to other debt buyers.[7] If in-house collection attempts were made, the debt buyers were asked to produce data regarding accounts that consumers disputed, including whether the debt buyers provided the consumer with verification of the debts and whether they resold disputed accounts.[8]

Because some debt buyers resell some accounts they have purchased to other debt buyers, the orders required that the debt buyers produce the same types of data for transactions in which they sold debt as for transactions in which they bought debt.[9] The debt buyers were asked to produce the information they provided to secondary debt buyers at the time of purchase and after the time of purchase for a sample of portfolios they purchased during the period March 2009

---

[5] *Id.* at Specification II.D.1. To reduce the burden on responding debt buyers, the Commission accepted information from a sample of portfolios in lieu of producing information about all portfolios during that time period.

[6] *Id.* at Specification II.D.2. To reduce the burden on responding debt buyers, the Commission accepted information from a sample of portfolios in lieu of producing information about all portfolios during that time period.

[7] *Id.* at Specification II.A.3.

[8] *Id.* at Specification II.A.5.

[9] *Id.* at Specification II.E, II.F, and II.G.

through August 2009.[10]

---

[10] *Id.* at Specification II.G.2 and II.G.3. To reduce the burden on responding debt buyers, the Commission accepted information from a sample of portfolios in lieu of producing information about all portfolios during that time period.

**UNITED STATES OF AMERICA
BEFORE THE FEDERAL TRADE COMMISSION**

COMMISSIONERS: Jon Leibowitz, Chairman
                        Pamela Jones Harbour
                        William E. Kovacic
                        J. Thomas Rosch

FTC Matter No. P104801

ORDER TO FILE A SPECIAL REPORT

Pursuant to a resolution of the Federal Trade Commission (henceforth the "Commission" or the "FTC") dated December 16, 2009, titled *"Resolution Directing the Use of Compulsory Process to Study the Practice of Debt Buying,"* a copy of which is enclosed, [COMPANY] is ordered to file a Special Report with the Commission no later than February 25, 2010, containing the information and documents specified herein.

The Special Report should restate each item of this Order with which the corresponding answer is identified. The Report is required to be subscribed and sworn to by an official of [COMPANY] who has prepared or supervised the preparation of the Report from books, records, correspondence, and/or other data and material in its possession, custody or control. If any Specification cannot be answered fully, provide the information that is available and explain in what respects and why the answer is incomplete.

Please provide the data, information, and documents requested in the following Specifications, consistent with the Definitions and Instructions attached as Exhibit A.

SPECIFICATIONS

I. Background Information. Please provide the following information:

    A. Identify by full name, business address, telephone number, and official capacity, the officers of the Company who have prepared or supervised the preparation of its response to this Order.

    B. Identify the Company by full name, address, and state of incorporation.

II. Interrogatories and Document Requests.

    A. Debt Buyer Business Information

        1. For each of the years 2006, 2007, and 2008, state the Company's annual total revenues earned from (a) collecting on purchased debt, (b) selling debt portfolios, and (c) other debt collection-related activities; and state the Company's annual total profits earned from (a) collecting on purchased debt, (b) selling debt portfolios, and (c) other debt collection-related activities.

        2. State the number of portfolios the Company purchased during each of the years 2006, 2007 and 2008.

        3. For each portfolio the Company purchased between July 1, 2006, and June 30, 2009, provide:
            a. A unique numerical identification number;
            b. The portfolio seller's name;
            c. The number of consumer accounts in the portfolio;
            d. The types of accounts included (e.g., credit card, medical, auto, etc.);
            e. The amount the Company paid for the portfolio;
            f. The average and standard deviations of the face value of accounts;
            g. The average and standard deviations of the age of accounts;
            h. The number and average face value of accounts the Company attempted to collect using in-house collectors;
            i. The number and average face value of accounts the Company sent to collection agencies or collection law firms on a contingency basis;
            j. The number and average face value of accounts the Company sold without first attempting to collect;
            k. The number and average face value of accounts which were not sold and for which no collection effort was attempted;
            l. The number and average face value of accounts that have been:
                (1) owned only by the original creditor prior to the Company's purchase;
                (2) owned by one debt buyer prior to the Company's purchase;
                (3) owned by two debt buyers prior to the Company's purchase; and
                (4) owned by three or more debt buyers prior to the Company's purchase;
            m. The number and average face value of accounts that were:

(1) not placed with any contingency collectors prior to purchase by the Company;

(2) placed with one contingency collector prior to purchase by the Company;

(3) placed with two contingency collectors prior to purchase by the Company; and

(4) placed with three or more contingency collectors prior to purchase by the Company.

Provide documents showing how the Company arrived at the information provided in response to this specification.

4. Describe the Company's policies and procedures concerning whether to add interest, fees, or other charges to the amount owed on the accounts it purchases. If interest, fees, or other charges are added, describe how the Company determines how much to add to the balance of an account. Provide all manuals and other documents that relate to these policies and procedures.

5. For each portfolio the Company purchased between July 1, 2006, and June 30, 2009, provide:
   a. The portfolio identification number assigned in 3a;
   b. The number and average face value of accounts the Company attempted to collect for which the consumer disputed all of the debt in writing;
   c. The number and average face value of accounts the Company attempted to collect for which the consumer disputed part of the debt in writing;
   d. The number and average face value of accounts the Company attempted to collect for which the consumer disputed all or part of the debt orally;
   e. The number and average face value of accounts for which the Company provided written verification of the debt to the consumer after receiving a written dispute;
   f. The number and average face value of accounts for which the Company provided written verification of the debt to the consumer after receiving an oral dispute;
   g. The number and average face value of accounts that were disputed which the Company sold without sending written verification to the consumer;
   h. The number and average face value of accounts that were disputed which the Company sold after sending written verification to the consumer;
   i. The number and average face value of accounts that were disputed in writing and that were:
      (1) owned only by the original creditor prior to purchase by the Company;
      (2) owned by one debt buyer prior to purchase by the Company; and
      (3) owned by two or more debt buyers prior to purchase by the Company;
   j. The number and average face value of disputed debts that had been:
      (1) owned only by the original creditor prior to purchase by the Company and for which the Company sent written verification to consumers;
      (2) owned by one debt buyer prior to purchase by the Company and for which the Company sent written verification to consumers; and
      (3) owned by two or more debt buyers prior to purchase by the Company and for which the Company sent written verification to consumers;
   k. The average number of phone numbers called per account; and

l.   The average number of incorrect parties reached per account.

Provide documents showing how the Company arrived at the information provided in response to this specification.

6.   Identify all purchasers to whom the Company has resold accounts, and state how many accounts the Company sold to each purchaser. For each purchaser, state the number of accounts the Company sold for which the consumer paid to the Company (a) a portion of the amount owed, and (b) none of the amount owed. Provide documents showing how the Company arrived at the information provided in response to this specification.

B.   Purchasing of Debt

1.   Describe the process through which sellers create portfolios to be offered for sale, including whether accounts in portfolios are grouped by age of debt, by type of creditor, by similarly sized accounts, by other categories, or by a combination of these categories.

2.   Describe the process through which the Company learns of portfolios of consumer accounts being offered for sale. Provide all advertising and other marketing materials relating to any portfolios the Company has purchased or bid on.

3.   Describe the information and documents that the Company obtains or obtains access to from sellers before the Company decides whether to purchase a portfolio of consumer accounts. For every portfolio that the Company purchased or bid on, provide all information and documentation relating to the portfolio that the Company obtained or obtained access to before deciding whether to bid on or purchase it.

4.   Describe the process the Company uses to evaluate a portfolio before determining whether to bid on or purchase it. Provide all manuals and other documents relating to this decision-making process.

C.   Contracts to Purchase Debt

1.   Describe the agreements in which the Company is required to purchase accounts from debt sellers on a regular basis, often called "forward-flow agreements," including the process through which the Company chooses to enter into a forward-flow agreement. To the extent the Company is not required to purchase every portfolio that a seller offers as part of a forward-flow agreement, describe how the Company selects which of these portfolios to purchase, including a description of the documents that the sellers provide or provide access to before the Company decides whether to purchase a portfolio. Provide copies of the forward-flow agreements to which the Company is a party, and provide the portfolio identification numbers of the portfolios associated with each contract.

2. Describe each of the different types of contracts that the Company has used when buying consumer accounts. Provide a copy of all contracts that the Company has used to buy consumer accounts, and list the portfolio identification numbers of the portfolios associated with each contract.

D. Information About Purchased Debt

1. Describe the information and documents about a portfolio that the Company obtains or obtains access to from the seller at the time the Company purchases a portfolio. To the extent that the information varies depending on the type of debt in the portfolio (*e.g.*, credit card, auto loan, or medical debt), describe the differences, including whether the completeness or reliability of documentation and other information varies by type of debt, by original creditor, or by some other consideration. For each portfolio purchased during the period March 2009 through August 2009, provide: (a) the portfolio identification number; and (b) all information about the portfolio the Company obtained or obtained access to from the seller at the time of purchase, including the schedule of accounts and the bill of sale.

2. Describe the terms and conditions under which the Company is permitted to obtain or obtain access to additional information from the seller about accounts in a portfolio after the time of purchase. For each portfolio the Company purchased during the period March 2009 through August 2009, provide: (a) the portfolio identification number; and (b) all additional information the Company has obtained or obtained access to from the seller since the time of purchase.

E. Selling of Debt

1. For each portfolio the Company has sold, provide: (a) the name of the buyer; (b) the number of consumer accounts; (c) the types of debt included (e.g., credit card, medical, auto, etc.); (d) the total face value of the accounts in the portfolio; (e) the amount the buyer paid; and (f) the average face value of the accounts in the portfolio. Provide documents showing how the Company arrived at the information provided in response to this specification.

2. Describe the Company's policies and procedures for determining whether to resell to another debt buyer accounts on which the Company has not collected any amount. Provide all manuals and other documents relating to these policies and procedures.
3. Describe the Company's policies and procedures for determining whether to resell to another debt buyer accounts on which the Company has collected some, but not all, of the debt. Provide all manuals and other documentation that relate to these policies and procedures.

F. Contracts to Sell Debt

1. Describe each of the different types of contracts that the Company has used when selling consumer accounts. Provide a copy of all contracts that the Company has

used to sell consumer accounts. To the extent that some contracts are identical to each other except for the names of the other parties to the contract, provide only one of the contracts and provide a list of the other parties on those contracts that the Company is not producing in response to this request.

G. Information About Sold Debt

1. Describe the terms and conditions under which a Secondary Debt Buyer can obtain or obtain access to documents and other information about an account from the Company or from the original creditor at the time the Secondary Debt Buyer purchases from the Company the portfolio containing the account. Provide all manuals and other documents that relate to these terms and conditions.

2. Describe the information and documents that the Company provides or provides access to Secondary Debt Buyers at the time it sells a portfolio. To the extent the information varies depending on the type of debt in the portfolio (*e.g.*, credit card, auto loan, or medical debt), describe the differences. For each portfolio the Company sold during the period March 2009 through August 2009, provide (a) the portfolio identification number; and (b) all information the Company provided or provided access to the Secondary Debt Buyer at the time of purchase, including the schedule of accounts and the bill of sale.

3. Describe the terms and conditions under which a Secondary Debt Buyer can obtain or obtain access to documents and other information about an account from the Company or the original creditor after the time of purchase from the Company. Provide all manuals and other documents that relate to these terms and conditions. For each portfolio that the Company sold to a Secondary Debt Buyer during the period March 2009 through August 2009 and for which the Company has provided or provided access to documents and other information to the Secondary Debt Buyer after the time of purchase, provide: (a) the portfolio identification number; and (b) all documents and other information the Company provided, directly or indirectly, to the Secondary Debt Buyer after the time of purchase.

4. Describe the terms and conditions under which a Tertiary Debt Buyer can obtain or obtain access to documents and other information about an account from the Company or the original creditor. Provide all manuals and other documents that relate to these terms and conditions. For each account for which the Company has provided or provided access to Tertiary Debt Buyers in 2009, provide: (a) the portfolio identification number of the portfolio in which the account was sold to the Secondary Debt Buyer; and (b) all documents and other information the Company provided, directly or indirectly.

H. Information About Computer Systems

1. Identify and describe all computer databases or other software used to maintain, update, and analyze records of consumer accounts, collection calls, collection payments, and other collection data. Provide:
   a. The name of the database;
   b. The time period during which the database was used;
   c. A list of the tables in each database and a list of the data fields in each table;
   d. Whether the database was purchased, developed in-house, or custom-designed for the company;
   e. If the database was purchased, provide the name of the manufacturer and seller;
   f. If the database was custom-designed, provide the name of the company or parties that designed it;
   g. The name of any relational database programs (such as Oracle, Access, or MySQL) used as a back-end in the database software; and
   h. Any manuals that apply to the database software.

2. Describe the process used to ensure that debt information arrives in a useable form when purchasing portfolios of debt, and describe how data about debts is entered into the Company's database.
   a. For each portfolio of debt purchased by the Company, describe the file format in which debt data was provided from the debt seller.

3. Identify and describe all computer programs (aside from databases) that the Company uses in the collection of debts. Include programs such as dialers and skip tracing software.
   a. Provide the time period during which each program was used;
   b. If the software was purchased, provide the name of the software manufacturer and the seller; and
   c. If the software was custom-designed, provide the name of the company or parties that designed it.

4. Specifically identify and describe the Company's policies and procedures for:
   a. Recording Consumer Communications;
   b. Updating relevant databases in response to Consumer Communications; and
   c. Responding to Consumer Communications.

EXHIBIT A

DEFINITIONS AND INSTRUCTIONS

For the purposes of this Order, the following specific definitions and instructions apply unless otherwise specified:

DEFINITIONS

1. "All" means "any and all." "Any" means "any and all."

2. "And" as well as "or" shall be construed both conjunctively and disjunctively, as necessary, in order to bring within the scope of any Specifications all information that otherwise might be construed to be outside the scope of the Specification.

3. "Company" or "You" means [COMPANY] and all directors, officers, employees, agents, consultants, and other persons working for or on behalf of [COMPANY].

4. "Consumer Communication" means
   a. A written request from a consumer that the company cease communication;
   b. A written notification from a consumer that a debtor being sought in collection calls to the consumer is not at the telephone number being called and/or that the consumer has no knowledge of the debtor's location;
   c. An oral request from a consumer that the company cease communication; or
   d. An oral notification from a consumer that a debtor being sought in collection calls to the consumer is not at the telephone number being called and/or that the consumer has no knowledge of the debtor's location.

5. "Contingency collector" means a debt collection agency or collection law firm that collects on behalf of another entity and receives from the agency a contingency fee based on the amount of money the agency or firm collects.

6. "Describe" means to provide information sufficient to allow a reasonable and complete understanding of the substance of any policy, procedure, or other referenced matter. Where "describe" is specified, if summaries, compilations, lists, or synopses are available that are sufficient to provide a reasonable and complete understanding of the requested information, these should be provided in lieu of the underlying documents.

7. "Document" means the complete original and any non-identical copy (whether different from the original because of notations on the copy or otherwise), regardless of origin or location, of any written, typed, printed, transcribed, taped, recorded, filmed, punched, computer-stored, or graphic matter of every type and description, however and by whomever prepared, produced, disseminated, or made, including but not limited to any advertisement, book, pamphlet, periodical, contract, correspondence, file, invoice, memorandum, note, telegram, report, record, handwritten note, working paper, routing slip, chart, graph, paper, index, map, tabulation, manual, guide, outline, script, abstract, history, calendar, diary, agenda, minute, code book, electronic mail, and computer material (including print-outs, cards, magnetic or electronic tapes, discs, and such codes or instructions as will transform such computer materials into easily understandable form).

8. "Each" shall be construed to include "every," and "every" shall be construed to include "each."

9. "Including," "e.g.," and "such as" mean "including but not limited to."

10. "Portfolio" means a collection of consumer accounts that are sold as a group.

11. "Relating to" or "with respect to" any given subject means in whole or in part constituting, containing, concerning, embodying, reflecting, discussing, explaining, describing, analyzing, identifying, stating, referring to, dealing with, or in any way pertaining to.

12. "Secondary Debt Buyer" means a debt buyer that purchases a portfolio or portfolios from the Company.

13. "Tertiary Debt Buyer" means a debt buyer that purchases a portfolio or portfolios from a Secondary Debt Buyer.

INSTRUCTIONS

1. **Submission Information.** Please send responses to Margaret Patterson, Bureau of Economics, Federal Trade Commission, 601 New Jersey Avenue, N.W., Mail Drop NJ-4136, Washington, D.C. 20580. Ms. Patterson may be reached at (202) 326-3472. A representative of [COMPANY] does not need to personally deliver the responses. Each Specification of this Order contemplates a complete search of all of [COMPANY]'s files and any other materials otherwise in [COMPANY]'s possession, custody, or control. Responsive material should be submitted on a rolling basis, with those documents and/or files that constitute a complete response to a given Specification to be submitted as soon as possible prior to the final return date.

    a. Prior to production of any of the materials requested in this Order, [COMPANY] should confer with Commission staff to ensure that the data and documents to be produced in response to this Order are consistent with the staff's understanding of what each data item represents. Additionally, if [COMPANY] wishes to produce data or documents in a format other than one of those specified in this Order, please contact Commission staff to discuss this option before doing so.

2. **Applicable Time Period:** Unless otherwise specified, provide all information and documents for the period from July 1, 2006, up to and including June 30, 2009.

3. **Time for Compliance.** Any request to extend the time for compliance with this Order will be resolved under Commission Rule of Practice 2.12(b). 16 C.F.R. § 2.12(b).

4. **Material Withheld, Claims of Privilege.** If [COMPANY] withholds all or any portion of any responsive piece of data or document for any reason, including an asserted privilege, state in writing individually for each piece of data or document: its type, title, subject matter, and date; the names, addresses, positions, and organizations of each author and recipient; and the specific grounds for claiming that the document is privileged, as well as facts sufficient to support such a claim. For each piece of responsive data, or document, withheld under a claim that it constitutes or contains attorney work product, also state whether the document was prepared in anticipation of litigation or for trial and, if so, identify the anticipated litigation or trial upon which the assertion is based.

5. **Data/Documents Lost or Destroyed.** If data or documents responsive to a particular Specification no longer exist, but are known to have been in existence, please: (1) state the circumstance under which they were lost or destroyed; (2) describe the data or documents to the fullest extent possible; (3) identify persons having knowledge of the content of such documents; and (4) provide a statement of the data or document retention policies.

6. **Verb Tenses, Plural vs. Singular.** In each Specification, the present tense shall be construed to include the past tense, and the past tense shall be construed to include the present tense. The singular shall be construed to include the plural, and the plural shall be construed to include the singular.

7. **Document Organization.** This set of instructions should be followed for all document submissions, whether submitted in electronic form or in hard copy:

   a. All documents submitted in response to Specifications should be Bates-stamped or otherwise sequentially numbered.
   b. Provide a master list showing all documents produced, identified by document Bates or control number, name of the person, department, and, if applicable, the entity (e.g., subsidiary or affiliate) that created the document, and the Specification number to which the document is responsive.
   c. Documents that may be responsive to more than one Specification of this Order need not be submitted more than once; however, please indicate, for each document submitted, each Specification to which the document is responsive. If any documents responsive to this Order have been previously supplied to the Commission, in lieu of re-supplying those materials it is permissible to identify the document(s) previously provided and the date of submission.

8. **Submission of Electronically Stored Information.** The following guidelines refer to any electronically stored information ("ESI") the Company submits. But, before submitting any ESI, You must confirm with the FTC that the proposed formats and media types that contain ESI will be acceptable to the government.

   a. Magnetic and other electronic media types accepted

      i. CD-R CD-ROMs formatted to ISO 9660 specifications.
      ii. DVD-ROM for Windows-compatible personal computers.
      iii. IDE and EIDE hard disk drives, formatted in Microsoft Windows-compatible, uncompressed data.

      iv. Note: Other types of tape media used for archival, backup, or other purposes such as 4mm & 8mm DAT and other cassette, mini-cartridge, cartridge, and DAT/helical scan tapes, DLT, or other types of media will be accepted only with prior approval.

   b. File and record formats

i. <u>E-mail</u>: The FTC accepts MS Outlook PST files, MS Outlook MSG files, and Lotus Notes NSF files. <u>Any other electronic submission of email will be accepted only with prior approval.</u>

ii. <u>Scanned Documents</u>: Image submissions accepted with the understanding that unreadable images will be resubmitted in original, hard copy format in a timely manner. Scanned Documents must adhere to the following specifications:

    (a) All images must be multi-page, 300 DPI - Group IV TIFF files named for the beginning bates number.

    (b) If the full text of the Document is available, that should be provided as well. The text should be provided in one file for the entire Document or email, named the same as the first TIFF file of the Document with a *.TXT extension.

    (c) <u>Note</u>: Single-page, 300 DPI - Group IV TIFF files may be submitted <u>with prior approval</u> if accompanied by an acceptable load file such as a Summation or Concordance image load file which denotes the appropriate information to allow the loading of the images into a Document management system with all Documents breaks (document delimitation) preserved. OCR accompanying single-page TIFF submissions should be located in the same folder and named the same as the corresponding TIFF page it was extracted from, with a *.TXT extension.

iii. <u>Other ESI files</u>: The FTC accepts word processing Documents in ASCII text, WordPerfect version X3 or earlier, or Microsoft Word 2003 version or earlier. Spreadsheets should be in MS Excel 2003 (*.xls) version or earlier. Database files should be in MS Access 2003 or earlier. PowerPoint presentations may be submitted in MS PowerPoint 2003 or earlier. <u>Other proprietary formats for PC files should not be submitted without prior approval.</u> Files may be submitted using the compressed ZIP format to reduce size and ease portability. Adobe Acrobat PDF (*.pdf) may be submitted where the normal business practice storage method is PDF.

iv. <u>Note</u>: Database files may also be submitted <u>with prior approval</u> as delimited ASCII text files, with field names as the first record, or as fixed-length flat files with appropriate record layout. For ASCII text files, field-level documentation should also be provided and care taken so that delimiters and quote characters do not appear in the data. The FTC may require a sample of the data to be sent for testing.

c. Security

i. All submissions of ESI to the FTC must be free of computer viruses. In addition, any passwords protecting Documents or files must be removed or provided to the FTC.

ii. Magnetic media shall be carefully packed to avoid damage and must be clearly marked on the outside of the shipping container:

**MAGNETIC MEDIA -- DO NOT X-RAY
MAY BE OPENED FOR POSTAL INSPECTION.**

9. **Submission of Documents in Hard Copies.** Any hard copy documents or narrative responses shall be submitted as follows:

   a. The FTC accepts hard copies of documents where the normal business practice storage method for these documents is in such a format – and only if such documents are not maintained also in electronic form. Documents and/or narrative responses submitted in hard copy shall be submitted in sturdy cartons not larger than 1.5 cubic feet. Number each such box and mark each such box with corporate identification and the name(s) of the person(s) whose files are contained in the box.

   b. All hard copy documents responsive to these Specifications shall be produced in complete form, unredacted unless privileged, and in the order in which they appear in the Company's files (unless otherwise specified).

   c. Unless otherwise stated, legible photocopies may be submitted in lieu of original documents, provided that the originals are retained in their state at the time of service of this Order. Further, copies of original documents may be submitted in lieu of originals only if they are true, correct, and complete copies of the original documents. A complete copy of each document should be submitted even if only a portion of the document is within the terms of the Specification. The document shall not be edited, cut, or expunged, and shall include all covering letters, memoranda, transmittal slips, appendices, tables, or other attachments, and all other documents referred to in the document or attachments.

   d. Transport hard copies using a delivery method that offers a tracking service, such as UPS or FedEx, or the equivalent. If a courier is used, ensure that there are no stops between pickup and delivery.

10. **Sensitive Personally Identifiable Information.** If any material called for by these requests contains sensitive personally identifiable information or sensitive health information of any individual, please contact us to discuss whether it would be appropriate to redact the sensitive information. If that information will not be redacted, contact us to discuss ways of protecting the information during production, including encrypting any electronic copies of such material with encryption software such as SecureZip and providing the encryption key in a separate communication.

    For purposes of these requests, sensitive personally identifiable information includes: an individual's Social Security number alone; or an individual's name or address or phone number in combination with one or more of the following: date of birth, Social Security number, driver's license number or other state identification number, or a foreign country equivalent, passport number, financial account number, credit card number, or debit card number. Sensitive health information includes medical records and other individually identifiable health information relating to the past, present, or future physical or mental health or conditions of an individual, the provision of health care to an individual, or the past, present, or future payment for the provision of health care to an individual.

11. **Verification.** The attached verification form should be executed by the official supervising compliance with this request and notarized.

VERIFICATION

This response to the Order of the Federal Trade Commission for information, together with any and all attachments thereto, was prepared and assembled under my supervision. The information is, to the best of my knowledge, true, correct, and complete.

_____

TYPE OR PRINT NAME AND TITLE

_____

SIGNATURE

Subscribed and sworn to before me at the City of _____, State of _____, this _____ day of _____ 2009.

_____

Notary Public

My commission expires: _____.

By the direction of the Commission.

Jon Leibowitz
Chairman

SEAL

Date of Order: _____, 2009

The Special Report required by this Order,
or any inquiry concerning it, should be
addressed to the attention of:

Margaret Patterson
Bureau of Economics
Federal Trade Commission
601 New Jersey Ave., NW, NJ-4143
Washington, DC 20580
(202) 326-3472 (telephone)
(202) 326-3443 (facsimile)
mpatterson@ftc.gov

Thomas E. Kane
Division of Financial Practices
Bureau of Consumer Protection
Federal Trade Commission
601 New Jersey Ave., NW, NJ-3158
Washington, DC 20580
(202) 326-2304 (telephone)
(202) 326-3768 (facsimile)
tkane@ftc.gov

TECHNICAL APPENDIX B:
PORTFOLIO-LEVEL DATA ANALYSIS

Technical Appendix B: Portfolio-level Data Analysis

I.   Introduction

This technical appendix analyzes data submissions provided by debt buying companies in order to shed light on how the debt buying market operates. Specific questions that our analysis attempts to address include:

1. How are debt portfolios composed?

2. To what extent do debt buyers attempt to collect on time-barred debt?

3. What debt characteristics are predictive of disputes and the verification of disputes?

We provide details on all of the major steps taken in the corresponding analysis, including how the sample of debt buying companies was constructed, what statistical methods were used, and what were the main findings of this analysis.

II.   Data

For our analysis, we use portfolio-level data for each portfolio purchased by a sample of debt buying companies between July 1, 2006 and June 20, 2009. The FTC sent 6(b) orders to nine debt buying firms.[1] Arrow Financial Services exited the debt buying business in the middle of our sampling time frame and did not have the ability to provide the requested data. Additionally, although FTC staff was generally aware of the business models of B-Line, LLC and eCAST Settlement Corp., we discovered the full extent to which they specialize in bankruptcy debts after receiving their responses to the 6(b) orders. Because of the particular

---

[1] These firms included: Asta Funding, Inc.; Arrow Financial Services, LLC; B-Line, LLC; eCAST Settlement Corp.; Encore Capital Group, Inc.; NCO Portfolio Management, Inc.; Portfolio Recovery Associates, LLC; Sherman Financial Group, LLC; and Unifund Corp.. Encore Capital is a holding company that does not purchase, sell, or collect debt. These functions are performed by Encore's subsidiaries, including Midland Credit Management (MCM), Inc. and Midland Funding, LLC. These subsidiaries voluntarily submitted data in response to the 6(b) order sent to Encore Capital.

practices of this specialized type of debt buyer, the bankruptcy debt buying firms did not have information responsive to those provisions of the 6(b) orders used in the analyses described in this appendix. As a result, these three firms were excluded from our sample.

The debt characteristics that are observed for each portfolio in the data include average debt age in months,[2] the standard deviation of debt age, the type of debt included in the portfolio (*e.g.*, credit card, auto loan, etc.), the number of debts sent to contingency collectors prior to purchase, whether the portfolio was acquired from the original creditor, and the purchase price of the portfolio.[3] The data also include information on the actions undertaken on the portfolios by the debt buyers after purchase and the number of accounts disputed by consumers. Our analysis is restricted to portfolios that are not missing information for any of these variables.[4]

It is important to note that the characteristics of the debts purchased by our sample are more likely to be reflective of debts purchased by other debt buyers of comparable size and with similar business practices than debts purchased by smaller debt buyers and those with different business practices. They are also more likely to be representative of debts sold within the period covered by the sampling timeframe of our investigation than debts sold in other time periods. They are not necessarily reflective of the debts purchased by smaller debt buying firms or by the overall industry.

---

[2] "Age" is defined as the time between debt charge-off and purchase. *See infra* p. B-6.

[3] The 6(b) orders did not request that debt buyers provide information on the acquisition date of portfolios or on the bankruptcy status of the accounts comprising each portfolio. Some firms did voluntarily provide this information for some or all of their portfolios. Although it would be appropriate to include these variables if data were available for all portfolios in the sample, including them for only part of the sample is not desirable because the corresponding conditional average estimates would be potentially misleading. Sensitivity analysis using available data on acquisition date and bankruptcy status produces results generally similar to those presented here for the debt characteristics consistently observed in the data.

[4] The six debt buyers submitted data from 3,418 portfolios. Of these, 19 were not included in our analysis of the determinants of debt price because of missing data.

III.   **Statistical Methods**

The debt buyers provided us with portfolio-level data that aggregate account-level information. However, our primary interest is in providing statistical evidence on the characteristics of accounts and on how such characteristics are predictive of debt buyer activities that are conducted at the account-level. Therefore, it is necessary to weight portfolio-level observations by the number of accounts in the portfolio in order to construct appropriate summary statistics for accounts.

Part of our investigation focuses on how individual accounts are packaged into portfolios. In order to address this particular question, we conduct an analysis of variance (ANOVA). According to the law of total variance:

$$\text{var}(x) = \text{var}(E[x \mid J]) + E[\text{var}(x \mid J)]$$

The first term is the part of the total variance of a debt characteristic, x, that is explained by the portfolio, J, to which the account is assigned. The second term is the part of total variance that is unexplained by portfolio designation. Using appropriate weights, we are able to calculate both terms for a select number of debt characteristics found in our data. We are then able to statistically test whether accounts appear to be grouped into portfolios by the debt characteristic. The formula for the corresponding one-way ANOVA F-test statistic is:

$$F = \frac{\text{explained variance}}{\text{unexplained variance}}$$

This F-statistic follows the F-distribution with $P - 1$, $N - P$ degrees of freedom under the null hypothesis, where P is the number of portfolios and N is the number of accounts. The null hypothesis in this case is that the assignment of accounts to portfolios is independent of the debt characteristic.

It is similarly necessary to appropriately weight portfolio-level observations for our analysis of how account characteristics predict debt buyer activities. One can model the expectation of a particular debt buyer activity or outcome, y, conditional on a vector of debt characteristics, X, as a linear function:

$$E[y_{ij} \mid X_{ij}] = \beta_0 + \beta_1 x_{ij}^{(1)} + \beta_2 x_{ij}^{(2)} + \cdots + \beta_k x_{ij}^{(K)}$$

where this function includes K unknown parameters, β, corresponding to each of the debt characteristics, and where j denotes the portfolio and i denotes the account in the portfolio. If this is the conditional linear expectation function (CEF) of the account-level microdata, it also holds that:

$$E[\bar{y}_j \mid \bar{X}_j] = \beta_0 + \beta_1 \bar{x}_j^{(1)} + \beta_2 \bar{x}_j^{(2)} + \cdots + \beta_k \bar{x}_j^{(K)}$$

where $\bar{y}_j$ and $\bar{X}_j$ are the average values of y and X for all accounts in portfolio j. Because sample moments converge to population moments, it follows that weighted least squares (WLS) estimation of the CEF on the grouped, or portfolio-level, data will produce estimates of CEF parameters that are consistent and equivalent to those that would be produced using account-level microdata.[5] In other words, we are able to estimate regression parameters that are relevant to an analysis of accounts even though we only have portfolio-level aggregate data.

Debt buyer activities observed in the data, such as whether a debt buyer attempts to collect a debt internally, can be thought of as binary variables (with a value of one symbolizing that the debt buyer attempted to collect on a particular debt and a value of zero symbolizing that it did not attempt to collect that debt). It follows that the conditional expectation of y is equivalent to the conditional probability that y is equal to one, or:

---

[5] For a more in depth discussion of regression analysis using grouped data, see Angrist, Joshua D. and Jorn-Steffen Pischke (2009). Mostly Harmless Econometrics: An Empiricist's Companion. Princeton University Press: Princeton and Oxford.

$$E[y_{ij} \mid X_{ij}] = \Pr[y_{ij} = 1 \mid X_{ij}]$$

Therefore, our WLS estimates can specifically be interpreted as parameter estimates from a linear probability model (LPM) based on account-level microdata. Because the data report only proportions for these binary variables at the portfolio level, this precludes the estimation of other binary dependent variable models, such as logit or probit models.[6]

Certain outcomes in our data are only relevant for a subset of accounts contained in each portfolio. For example, we observe whether an account is disputed if and only if the debt buyer attempted to collect on that account using internal methods. An issue with our data is that for some analyses we only observe average characteristics for all accounts within the portfolio, instead of the average characteristics for the *relevant* accounts. In mathematical terms we observe the sample equivalent of $E[x_{ij}^{(k)}]$ for each portfolio instead of $E[x_{ij}^{(k)} \mid d_{ij} = 1]$, where d_{ij} is a binary variable that indicates whether an account is relevant ($d_{ij} = 1$). In order to deal with this limitation of the data, we define the underlying characteristics of accounts, $x_{ij}^{(k)}$, as binary variables and then take advantage of the properties of conditional probabilities in order to suggest a way to impute the unobserved $E[x_{ij}^{(k)} \mid d_{ij} = 1]$ for each portfolio. Specifically, if the underlying characteristics of accounts, $x_{ij}^{(k)}$, are defined as binary variables, it holds that:

$$E[x_{ij}^{(k)} \mid d_{ij} = 1] = \Pr[x_{ij}^{(k)} = 1 \mid d_{ij} = 1]$$

Based on the definition of a conditional probability, it follows that:

$$\Pr[x_{ij}^{(k)} = 1 \mid d_{ij} = 1] = \Pr[d_{ij} = 1 \mid x_{ij}^{(k)} = 1] * \left[\frac{\Pr[x_{ij}^{(k)} = 1]}{\Pr[d_{ij} = 1]} \right]$$

---

[6] The benefit of LPM parameter estimates is that they are more easily interpretable than those derived from logit or probit models. However, the corresponding predicted probabilities of a LPM are not bounded between zero and one, as is the case with these other models.

The first term on the right hand side, $\Pr[d_{ij} = 1 \mid x_{ij}^{(k)} = 1]$, can be estimated using the data.[7] The sample equivalents for the numerator and denominator of the second term are observed directly from the data for each portfolio. Therefore, we construct imputed values of the average characteristics for all *relevant* accounts in each portfolio as is implied by the conditional probability definition by multiplying these estimated and observed terms. In the corresponding analyses, we bootstrap the standard errors of the predictor variables to address the fact that these variables are imputed instead of observed.

Finally, it is important to note that we include debt buyer fixed effects (*e.g.*, controls for debt buyer identity) in all of our regression models. This was primarily done to account for potential measurement error that might result from different reporting practices across debt buying firms. These fixed effects are also likely to account for unobserved debt characteristics, to the extent that debt buyers selectively purchase debts with different types of unobserved characteristics. Additionally, debt buyer fixed effects might capture differences in business practices across firms. Even with the inclusion of these fixed effects, we would argue that readers should exercise caution in interpreting our regression results as demonstrating causal relationships between debt account characteristics and the outcomes of interest (*e.g.*, price, likelihood of a disputed account being verified, etc.).

IV.   **Results**

IV.A Mean Sample Characteristics

Table B1 presents the mean characteristics of debt accounts purchased by our sample of debt buyers. Means are further broken out by the source of purchase - original creditors, debt

---

[7] As we have noted, LPM estimates of conditional probabilities are not necessarily bounded between zero and one. As part of our imputation algorithm, we include rules that top code predicted probabilities that are above one as equal to one and bottom code predicted probabilities below zero as equal to zero.

buyers, and all sources. The debt size and age distributions reported in the table were calculated by using the means and standard deviations reported by the debt buyers for each portfolio and assuming a gamma distribution. The calculated distributions for debt size and age (and the results of our subsequent analyses) are not significantly affected by this distributional assumption.

Debt buyers in our sample acquired the vast majority of their debt accounts (a little over 80 percent) from the original creditor. On average, debt buyers paid 4.0 cents for each dollar of debt. Almost 40 percent of these were credit card debts. Medical and telecommunication debts also comprised a considerable share of the debts that buyers acquired from original creditors. A little over a quarter of debts acquired from original creditors had a face value greater than one thousand dollars.

On average, debt buyers paid less for accounts acquired from other debt buyers than for accounts acquired from original creditors. This lower price likely reflects the fact that debt buyers selectively sell accounts that they acquire from original creditors and that they are more likely to sell accounts with lower expected yields (*i.e.*, accounts they were not able to collect). At the same time, this difference in price might be a result of the fact that resold debts are observably older, are more likely to have been previously sent to contingency collectors, and have slightly larger face values than those sold by original creditors (with these characteristics conveying to the purchaser a lower expected yield).

One concern with debt resale is that it might increase the likelihood that account information is lost as it is passed along from debt buyer to debt buyer (possibly as a result of repackaging accounts into new portfolios). However, from the limited data that we have on the completeness of account information, this does not appear to be the case.[8] Debt portfolios acquired from other debt buyers are less likely to be missing information on debt age and whether the account had previously been sent to contingency collectors.

IV.B Allocation of Debt Accounts to Portfolios

To evaluate how debt accounts are allocated to portfolios, we conducted an ANOVA of debt age and face value. We are able to conduct such an analysis because the data include both the within portfolio standard deviation and portfolio mean for these two debt characteristics. These variables, in turn, allow us to calculate the within and between portfolio components of the total variance of debt age and face value within our sample. The corresponding results are presented in **Table B2**. They suggest that accounts are grouped into portfolios by debt age. This result is highly statistically significant. Grouping of accounts into portfolios by debt age is apparent for portfolios sold by both original creditors and debt buyers. These results also hold when we separately consider different types of debt. While the data suggest that debt accounts in our sample are grouped by debt age, it is important to note that this relationship is not necessarily causal. We would see the same pattern in the data if those constructing portfolios used another criterion to group debt accounts that happened to be correlated with account age.

Conversely, we find that accounts are not grouped into portfolios by face value. This result holds for portfolios sold by both original creditors and debt buyers, as well as for different types of debt. It is possible that accounts are not grouped into portfolios by face value as a means of diversification in order to reduce the risk associated with the portfolio. We are not able to conduct a similar analysis for categorical variables, such as debt type. However, most of the debt buyer submissions listed one debt type instead of multiple types per portfolio, suggesting

---

[8] Analysis of the price paid for debt purchased from original creditors and resellers is consistent with this finding. *See infra* p. B-10.

that portfolios group accounts of similar debt types.

IV.C Determinants of Portfolio Price

To evaluate how different debt characteristics affect price, we conducted a regression analysis. These results are presented in **Table B3**. The regression model predicts a baseline average price per dollar of debt of 7.9 cents across all debt buyers in the sample. The baseline corresponds to a credit card debt less than 3 years old, acquired from the original creditor, with a face value less than one thousand dollars, and that had never been sent to a contingency collector. All of the reported coefficient estimates should be interpreted as the predicted difference in debt price relative to the baseline. For example, our regression estimates suggest that debt buyers pay on average 4.8 cents less per dollar of debt for debts that are 3 to 6 years old compared to debts less than 3 years old.

Debt buyers generally pay less for older debts. In particular, they pay effectively zero for accounts that are older than fifteen years.[9] Relative to credit card debt, debt buyers pay substantially more for mortgage debt (on average 48 cents per dollar of debt more) and less for other types of debt such as medical, telecommunications, and utility debt.[10] On average, debt buyers pay less for accounts that have been previously sent out to contingency collectors and for accounts missing information on past contingency collection attempts.

Interestingly, once we control for other debt characteristics, we find no statistically significant relationship between debt price and whether or not a debt is purchased from the original creditor. In other words, debt buyers appear to be willing to pay the same price for

---

[9] The negative coefficient on debt older than 15 years is larger than the base line estimate, seemingly indicating a negative price. However, a joint significance test indicates that the price is not significantly different than zero.

[10] The substantially higher price for mortgage debt may be due to the inclusion of some portfolios of performing mortgages purchased by the debt buyers.

otherwise similar debts regardless of whether they are sold by the original creditor or another debt buyer. The differences in the average price of debt purchased from the two sources, as shown in Table B1, is therefore most likely due to different observable characteristics of the debt.

If account information were lost as it was passed along from debt buyer to debt buyer, we would expect debt buyers to take this into account in their valuation of debts and to pay less for accounts acquired from other debt buyers. However, we do not see this in the regression results. Possible interpretations of this result are either that information loss is not prevalent or that it does not affect the expected yield of accounts. Alternatively, it could be the case that any negative effect of information loss on price is balanced by some positive effect of unobserved characteristics typical of debts resold by debt buyers.[11]

IV.D Determinants of Debt Buyer Collection Practices

In addition to information on debt characteristics and prices, the portfolio-level data provided by each debt buying company also contain information on actions undertaken by the debt buyer after the purchase of each portfolio, including: the number of accounts the debt buyer referred to an outside contingency collector, the number of accounts the debt buyer attempted to collect internally, the number of accounts the debt buyer attempted to collect internally that were subsequently disputed, and the number of disputed accounts that the debt buyer verified. In the sections that follow, we evaluate to what extent debt characteristics predict these outcomes.[12]

---

[11] Our subsequent analysis provides weak evidence that debts acquired from debt buyers are both less likely to be disputed and less likely to be verified if they are disputed. These two tendencies would likely have opposite effects on price.

[12] Two debt buying firms did not provide us with information on account disputes and dispute verification. Additionally, one of these did not provide us with information on account collection attempts, since it does not perform collection activities (which are handled by an affiliate or other collection companies). As a result, these firms are not included in the estimation samples for these corresponding analyses.

Table B4 presents a breakdown of debt buyer activity after they purchase a debt. Debt buyers attempted to collect on around 88 percent of the acquired debts in our sample. Collection measures include both internal collection efforts on the part of debt buyers as well as sending debts out to contingency collectors. The overall collection rate is the same both for debts acquired from the original creditor and for those acquired from another debt buyer. However, debt buyers are more likely to rely on internal collection efforts when attempting to collect on an account acquired from another debt buyer. In a small number of cases (4.5 percent of all acquired debts), buyers resell accounts without attempting to collect on them. The majority of these resold accounts are debts purchased from the original creditor.

To evaluate how different debt characteristics affect the likelihood that buyers attempt different collection methods, we conducted a series of regression analyses. These results are presented in **Table B5**. The regression models predict that debt buyers attempt to internally collect 64 percent of accounts with baseline characteristics and send 78 percent of accounts out to contingency collectors.[13] Again, the baseline corresponds to a credit card debt less than 3 years old, acquired from the original creditor, with a face value less than one thousand dollars, and that had never been sent to a contingency collector. Debt buyers are less likely to try to internally collect on debts that were not acquired from the original creditor and on accounts missing information on debt age. They are also substantially more likely to attempt to internally collect mortgage debts and substantially less likely to send medical and utility debts to contingency collectors relative to credit card debts.

To what extent do debt buyers collect on time-barred debts, that is, debt that is outside the statute of limitations? While an important policy question, it is also a difficult question to

---

[13] It is important to note that these two outcomes are not mutually exclusive.

answer given the limitations of our data. Specifically, whether a debt is time-barred depends on the applicable statute of limitations. However, our data only include information on debt age and does not identify the relevant statute of limitations for individual debts. Nonetheless, information about the statute of limitations that states generally apply permits a rough assessment of how much of the debt in the study appears to be time-barred. There are no states that have a statute of limitations that is less than three years or greater than fifteen years. Most states have a statute of limitations between three and six years. Reviewing account-level records, it does appear that original creditors sell time-barred debts to debt buyers.[14] The ages of these time-barred debts ranged from just over three years to more than fifteen years. Our regression results suggest that debt buyers are more likely to both attempt to collect internally and send to contingency collectors debts that are six to fifteen years old. However, this result could reflect that debt buyers are more likely to focus collection efforts on debts that are approaching their statute of limitations, instead of suggesting that they are more likely to try to collect on time-barred debts.

Debts that are very likely to be time-barred (*i.e.*, older than fifteen years) are extremely rare, comprising less than one percent of our sample.[15] In the regression analysis of the collection activities of debt buyers, the standard errors that correspond to this category are quite large. In other words, our estimated collection rates for these very old debts are quite imprecise. However, the results of this analysis suggest that debt buyers do attempt to internally collect at

---

[14] Debt buyers submitted examples of final purchase data files for select portfolios acquired from original creditors. These data files included account-level information on debt age, debt type, and state of issue that allowed us to determine whether a debt account was past the statute of limitations. The selected portfolios are not necessarily representative of the full set of portfolios included in our sample. In addition, the sample of these selected portfolios was too small to conduct an independent statistical analysis of the corresponding data files.

[15] It is possible that the statute of limitations may have been tolled for some of these debts, for example, because the debt was part of a bankruptcy.

least some of these accounts. According to our estimates, debt buyers attempt to collect on debts that are older than fifteen years at least 29 percent of the time (based on the lower bound of a 95 percent confidence interval calculated for the estimated coefficient for debt older than 15 years). Conversely, it does not appear that debt buyers send these very old debts to contingency collectors based on this analysis (*i.e.*, we cannot reject the claim that debt buyers do not send any of these very old debts to contingency collectors).

IV.E Determinants of Consumer Disputes

As previously highlighted, debt buyers may attempt to collect on purchased debt through either internal collection efforts, sending accounts out to contingency collectors, or some combination of both. In our data, we only observe disputes for accounts that the debt buyer tried to collect internally.[16] Approximately 3.2 percent of the accounts that the debt buyers in our sample attempted to internally collect were subsequently disputed. We have no information on the incidence of disputes when collections are outsourced to contingency collectors. The collection methods that debt buyers choose to employ likely depend on their expectations about whether or not a given debt will be disputed. Therefore, our analysis of disputes arising from internal collection attempts is not necessarily informative with regards to disputes potentially arising from other types of collection activity.

To evaluate how different debt characteristics predict the likelihood that the consumer disputes a debt that the debt buyer is trying to internally collect, we conducted a regression analysis. These results are presented in **Table B6**.[17] The regression model suggests that

---

[16] As noted above, data on disputes and verification were submitted by four of the surveyed debt buyers.

[17] Because of the extremely small number of accounts with ages above fifteen years that received a collection attempt by debt buyers, the "15+ years" category was collapsed into the "6+ to 15 years" category for the estimation of the dispute rate and verification rate models.

consumers dispute around 0.3 percent of debts with baseline characteristics, with this amount not being statistically different than zero. Debts previously sent to contingency collectors are more likely to be disputed while consumer loan debts are less likely to be disputed relative to credit card debt. Conversely, we find no statistically significant relationship between a debt's age or face value and the likelihood that it is disputed. Dispute rates for debts purchased directly from the original creditor are not statistically significantly different from those purchased from other debt buyers.

In general, the observed debt characteristics (*e.g.*, age, face value, etc.) are not strong predictors of whether or not a debt subject to internal collection efforts is subsequently disputed. Debt characteristics explain only 36 percent of the variation in this outcome. Conversely, these same characteristics are highly predictive of debt buyer initiated actions, such as purchase price, whether a debt is subject to internal collection efforts, and whether a disputed debt is verified. Specifically, debt characteristics explain between 65 and 82 percent of the variation in these outcomes. It is important to note that it is the consumer that ultimately decides whether or not to respond to a collection attempt by disputing the debt. Therefore, it is likely that debtor characteristics (which we do not observe) are important determinants of disputes. Alternatively, it could be the case that observable debt characteristics are just not good predictors of whether a debt is in fact valid and that debt validity, which we do not observe, drives disputes.

IV.F Determinants of Disputed Debt Verification

Debt buyers successfully verify a little over half of disputed debts.[18] **Table B7** presents a breakdown of debt buyer activity after a debt that they attempted to internally collect was subsequently disputed. The verification rate is substantially higher for debts acquired from the

---

[18] If a dispute is not successfully verified, the data do not distinguish between whether the debt buyer did not attempt to verify the disputed debt or whether the debt buyer attempted to and failed to verify the debt account.

original creditor than for those acquired from another debt buyer. It is important to note that whether a dispute is successfully verified is self-reported by the debt buyer. However even if debt buyers overstate their ability to successfully verify disputed debts, the data still suggest that a very small fraction of all disputed debts (less than 3 percent) are subsequently resold.[19]

Table B8 presents a regression analysis of how well different debt characteristics predict the likelihood that a disputed debt is subsequently verified.[20] The regression model predicts that debt buyers verify almost 60 percent of disputed debts with baseline characteristics.[21] Many debt types have lower verification rates than credit card debt, particularly medical, telecommunications, and utility debt. Older debts are substantially less likely to be verified.

Our results also suggest that debts acquired from other debt buyers are around seven percentage points less likely to be verified (even after we account for the direct effect of debt age). However, this effect is only marginally statistically different from zero. This finding is weakly consistent with the idea that debt buyers lose some level of access to the information necessary for debt verification when they do not purchase debts from the original creditor.

---

[19] It is important to note that only two debt buyers submitted information relating to the sale of disputed debt.

[20] Because of the extremely small number of accounts with face values above twenty thousand dollars that received a collection attempt by debt buyers and that were subsequently disputed, the "20+ thousand dollar" category was collapsed into the "5-20 thousand dollar" category for the estimation of the verification rate model.

[21] The estimation algorithm resulted in all of the portfolios of one debt buyer being dropped from the estimation, leaving three debt buyers in the sample.

V. **Tables**

Table B1:   <u>Sample Characteristics of Debts Purchased by Six Debt Buyers</u>

Debt Characteristics	Debt Acquired from:		
	Original Creditor	Debt Buyer	All Sellers
Average Price Per Dollar of Debt	$0.043	$0.029	$0.040
Debt Age:			
0 to 3 years	75.2%	37.9%	68.2%
3+ to 6 years	16.3%	32.1%	19.3%
6+ to 15 years	7.5%	27.5%	11.3%
15+ years	0.4%	2.6%	0.8%
Not Reported	0.6%	0.0%	0.5%
Debt Face Value:			
0 to 1 thousand dollars	72.5%	67.4%	71.5%
1+ to 5 thousand dollars	20.0%	25.2%	21.0%
5+ to 20 thousand dollars	7.0%	6.7%	6.9%
20+ thousand dollars	0.5%	0.7%	0.5%
Account Type:			
Auto Loans	1.4%	18.5%	4.6%
Consumer Loans	1.5%	0.1%	1.2%
Credit Cards	36.4%	49.0%	38.8%
Medical	33.4%	0.0%	27.1%
Mortgages	0.0%	0.0%	0.0%
Overdraft	0.2%	0.0%	0.2%
Telecommunications	16.3%	9.1%	15.0%
Utility	2.2%	0.0%	1.7%
Other	8.7%	23.4%	11.5%
Previously Sent to Contingency Collector	47.8%	57.5%	49.6%
Previously Sent to Contingency Collector: Not Reported	47.1%	31.7%	44.2%
Not Acquired from Original Creditor	0.0%	100.0%	18.8%
# of Portfolio Observations	3,036	363	3,399
# of Accounts	61,534,019	14,281,636	75,815,655

Notes: All percentages are of purchased debt accounts. The distributions of debt age and face value were calculated assuming a gamma distribution characterized by the portfolio average and standard deviation of these variables.

Table B2: <u>**Analysis of Variance of Select Account Characteristics**</u>

Account Characteristics	Debt Acquired from:		
	Original Creditor	Debt Buyer	All Sellers
<u>Debt Age:</u>			
% of Variance Explained by Portfolio Assignment	68.4%	79.5%	75.5%
One-way ANOVA:			
F-statistic	2.17	3.88	3.08
P-value	0.0000***	0.0000***	0.0000***
<u>Debt Face Value:</u>			
% of Variance Explained by Portfolio Assignment	30.6%	1.7%	13.5%
One-way ANOVA:			
F-statistic	0.44	0.02	0.16
P-value	1.0000	1.0000	1.0000
# of Portfolio Observations	3,036	363	3,399
# of Accounts	61,534,019	14,281,636	75,815,655

Notes: The null hypothesis of the one-way ANOVA F-test is that assignment of accounts to portfolios is independent of the account characteristic. Statistical significance is denoted by "***" when significant at the 1% level, "**" when significant at the 5% level, and "*" when significant at the 10% level.

Table B3:   Regression Model of Purchase Price Per Dollar of Debt

Variables	Coeff.	Std. Error	
Baseline Price Per Dollar	**$0.079**	**$0.008**	***
Debt Age:			
3+ to 6 years	-$0.048	$0.005	***
6+ to 15 years	-$0.057	$0.006	***
15+ years	-$0.092	$0.027	***
Not Reported	$0.012	$0.037	
Debt Face Value:			
1+ to 5 thousand dollars	$0.002	$0.015	
5+ to 20 thousand dollars	-$0.023	$0.024	
20+ thousand dollars	-$0.066	$0.183	
Account Type:			
Auto Loans	-$0.011	$0.007	
Consumer Loans	-$0.011	$0.005	**
Medical	-$0.030	$0.006	***
Mortgages	$0.479	$0.169	***
Overdraft	-$0.011	$0.008	
Telecommunications	-$0.017	$0.006	***
Utility	-$0.036	$0.008	***
Other	-$0.030	$0.005	***
Previously Sent to Contingency Collector	-$0.014	$0.003	***
Previously Sent to Contingency Collector: Not Reported	-$0.016	$0.004	***
Not Acquired from Original Creditor	$0.004	$0.004	
R^2		0.65	
# of Portfolio Observations		3,399	
Total Face Value of All Accounts		$114,051,119,500	

Notes: While the model is estimated using portfolio aggregates, it is equivalent to a model estimated using account-level data. Model includes debt buyer fixed effects for the six firms included in the estimation sample. The baseline corresponds to a credit card debt that is less than 3 years old, acquired from the original creditor, with a face value less than one thousand dollars, and that had never been sent to a contingency collector. The predicted price per dollar is averaged across all debt buyers. Robust standard errors are reported. Statistical significance is denoted by "***" when significant at the 1% level, "**" when significant at the 5% level, and "*" when significant at the 10% level.

Table B4: **Breakdown of Debt Buyer Actions After Purchase**

	Debt Acquired from:		
	Original Creditor	Debt Buyer	All Sellers
Attempted to Collect:			
Internally Only	24.3%	37.3%	26.8%
w/ Contingency Collectors Only	32.0%	17.7%	29.2%
Internally & w/ Contingency Collectors	31.6%	33.0%	31.9%
All	*87.9%*	*88.0%*	*87.9%*
No Attempt to Collect:			
Subsequently Not Sold	7.3%	9.1%	7.6%
Subsequently Sold	4.9%	2.9%	4.5%
All	*12.1%*	*12.0%*	*12.1%*
# of Portfolio Observations	1,984	271	2,255
# of Accounts	28,076,421	6,853,756	34,930,177

Table B5: **Regression Models of the Probability that Debt Buyers Attempt Different Collection Methods**

Variables	Attempted to Collect Internally			Sent to Contingency Collector		
	Coeff.	Std. Error		Coeff.	Std. Error	
Baseline Probability of Collection Attempt	**64.10%**	**5.92%**	***	**77.96%**	**7.17%**	***
Debt Age:						
3+ to 6 years	16.14%	5.70%	***	-6.32%	7.59%	
6+ to 15 years	20.80%	6.17%	***	17.22%	8.57%	**
15+ years	36.71%	44.68%		-55.77%	31.66%	*
Not Reported	-8.09%	3.21%	**	-25.22%	16.61%	
Debt Face Value:						
1+ to 5 thousand dollars	-12.76%	11.79%		-23.57%	11.35%	**
5+ to 20 thousand dollars	1.87%	13.05%		-10.62%	15.22%	
20+ thousand dollars	-90.08%	73.90%		-51.36%	54.03%	
Account Type:						
Auto Loans	-36.85%	13.14%	***	-9.62%	5.71%	*
Consumer Loans	5.72%	4.97%		5.85%	4.00%	
Medical	-7.67%	5.32%		-32.18%	6.67%	***
Mortgages	149.65%	53.90%	***	-20.98%	45.85%	
Overdraft	-0.24%	4.89%		-7.67%	9.49%	
Telecommunications	24.22%	6.77%	***	-10.82%	4.51%	**
Utility	8.40%	3.81%	**	-23.76%	3.76%	***
Other	-9.04%	3.91%	**	-47.35%	10.90%	***
Previously Sent to Contingency Collector	-7.70%	3.66%	**	4.65%	2.60%	*
Previously Sent to Contingency Collector: Not Reported	-6.29%	4.63%		9.41%	3.18%	***
Not Acquired from Original Creditor	-13.22%	5.04%	***	2.80%	3.96%	
R^2		0.77			0.75	
# of Portfolio Observations		2,514			2,722	
# of Accounts		39,733,260			45,869,466	

Notes: Results are reported for separate regressions. Collection attempt outcomes are not mutually exclusive. While the models are estimated using portfolio aggregates, they are equivalent to linear probability models estimated using account-level data. Therefore, predicted probabilities are not constrained between 0 and 100 percent. Models include debt buyer fixed effects for the five firms included in the estimation sample. The baseline corresponds to a credit card debt that is less than 3 years old, acquired from the original creditor, with a face value less than one thousand dollars, and that had never been sent to a contingency collector. The predicted probability is averaged across all debt buyers. Robust standard errors are reported. Statistical significance is denoted by "***" when significant at the 1% level, "**" when significant at the 5% level, and "*" when significant at the 10% level.

Table B6: **Regression Model of the Probability of Accounts Receiving Internal Collection Attempts Being Subsequently Disputed**

Variables	Coeff.	Std. Error	
Baseline Probability of Dispute	**0.03%**	**2.51%**	
Debt Age:			
3+ to 6 years	0.68%	1.17%	
6+ years	-0.73%	1.25%	
Not Reported	4.28%	8.38%	
Debt Face Value:			
1+ to 5 thousand dollars	1.84%	3.26%	
5+ to 20 thousand dollars	1.23%	4.10%	
20+ thousand dollars	-0.35%	10.92%	
Account Type:			
Auto Loans	0.05%	1.81%	
Consumer Loans	-2.69%	1.32%	**
Medical	-0.27%	0.87%	
Mortgages	-10.04%	9.34%	
Overdraft	0.68%	4.97%	
Telecommunications	0.72%	0.76%	
Utility	-0.02%	0.64%	
Other	1.15%	1.12%	
Previously Sent to Contingency Collector	1.92%	0.48%	***
Previously Sent to Contingency Collector: Not Reported	1.09%	0.85%	
Not Acquired from Original Creditor	-1.34%	0.98%	
R^2		0.36	
# of Portfolio Observations		2,114	
# of Accounts		16,445,501	

Notes: While the model is estimated using portfolio aggregates, it is equivalent to a linear probability model estimated using account-level data. Therefore, predicted probabilities are not constrained between 0 and 100 percent. The model includes debt buyer fixed effects for the four firms included in the estimation sample. The baseline corresponds to a credit card debt that is less than 3 years old, acquired from the original creditor, with a face value less than one thousand dollars, and that had never been sent to a contingency collector. The predicted probability is averaged across all debt buyers. Because of the extremely small number of accounts with ages above fifteen years that received a collection attempt by debt buyers, the "15+ years" category was collapsed into the "6+ to 15 years" category for the estimation of the dispute rate and verification rate models. All regressors are imputed based on portfolio-level aggregates and the corresponding standard errors are bootstrapped accordingly. Statistical significance is denoted by "***" when significant at the 1% level, "**" when significant at the 5% level, and "*" when significant at the 10% level.

Table B7: __Breakdown of Debt Buyer Actions After Receiving Dispute__

	Debt Acquired from:		
	Original Creditor	Debt Buyer	All Sellers
Verified Debt:			
Subsequently Not Sold	53.3%	32.4%	48.8%
Subsequently Sold	2.5%	3.5%	2.5%
All	*55.7%*	*35.9%*	*51.3%*
Did Not Verify Debt:			
Subsequently Not Sold	43.9%	63.8%	48.3%
Subsequently Sold	0.4%	0.3%	0.4%
All	*44.3%*	*64.1%*	*48.7%*
# of Portfolio Observations	1,686	167	1,853
# of Accounts	553,587	159,721	713,308

Notes: The proportion of verified/non-verified debts that are subsequently sold is imputed based on the two firms that reported this information.

Table B8: **Regression Model of the Probability of Disputed Accounts Being Verified**

Variables	Coeff.	Std. Error	
Baseline Probability of Verification	**58.40%**	**2.89%**	***
Debt Age:			
3+ to 6 years	0.60%	3.85%	
6+ years	-22.33%	3.84%	***
Not Reported	11.43%	15.32%	
Debt Face Value:			
1+ to 5 thousand dollars	14.47%	37.67%	
5+ thousand dollars	-9.65%	18.11%	
Account Type:			
Auto Loans	0.18%	8.15%	
Consumer Loans	1.68%	3.12%	
Medical	-14.23%	4.00%	***
Mortgages	-21.93%	23.25%	
Overdraft	-4.14%	10.41%	
Telecommunications	-15.67%	3.34%	***
Utility	-8.55%	2.08%	***
Other	3.90%	2.73%	
Previously Sent to Contingency Collector	4.26%	1.83%	**
Previously Sent to Contingency Collector: Not Reported	6.42%	2.27%	***
Not Acquired from Original Creditor	-7.06%	3.74%	*
R^2		0.82	
# of Portfolio Observations		1,692	
# of Accounts		527,319	

Notes: While the model is estimated using portfolio aggregates, it is equivalent to a linear probability model estimated using account-level data. Therefore, predicted probabilities are not constrained between 0 and 100 percent. Model includes debt buyer fixed effects for the three firms included in the estimation sample. The baseline corresponds to a credit card debt that is less than 3 years old, acquired from the original creditor, with a face value less than one thousand dollars, and that had never been sent to a contingency collector. The predicted probability is averaged across all debt buyers. Because of the extremely small number of accounts with face values above twenty thousand dollars that received a collection attempt by debt buyers and that were subsequently disputed, the "20+ thousand dollar" category was collapsed into the "5-20 thousand dollar" category for the estimation of the verification rate model. All regressors are imputed based on portfolio-level aggregates and the corresponding standard errors are bootstrapped accordingly. Statistical significance is denoted by "***" when significant at the 1% level, "**" when significant at the 5% level, and "*" when significant at the 10% level.

TECHNICAL APPENDIX C:
ANALYSIS OF CONTRACTS

Technical Appendix C: Analysis of Contracts

1. Introduction

Contracts for the purchase and sale of consumer debts determine how consumer debt accounts pass from debt sellers to debt buyers, and some contract features may also affect debt buyers' collection practices. Accordingly, our investigation for this report included an examination of such contracts.

Surveyed firms were asked to provide us with copies of contracts associated with portfolios purchased during the period of inquiry. Respondents were permitted to produce one example of each type or variety of responsive contract, and the submissions suggest that "type or variety" was interpreted in a variety of ways, such that many of the sellers from whom debt buyers purchased portfolios were not represented among the contracts submitted.[1] The contracts submitted were not a random sample of contracts used throughout the industry, nor were they a random sample of each respondent's contracts. Consequently, we cannot say that the frequency with which particular contractual features of interest were found in the submission would also be found with that same frequency amongst all contracts used in the debt buying industry, or even amongst all contracts used by any respondent.[2] Nonetheless, the contract submissions yielded a rich variety of contractual terms and conditions, and we believe they have aided our understanding of how the debt buying industry works.

---

[1] Surveyed debt buyers submitted more than 5,000 portfolios of purchased debts and approximately 350 contracts.

[2] Accordingly, deliberately non-specific terms, such as "few," "some," "many," and "most," are used instead of percentage figures in the discussion below when referring to the frequency with which certain contract features are present in the submission of contracts. The use of percentage measures might tempt some readers of this report to make projections to the industry where none is warranted. Additionally, since we are reporting on contracts submitted by a relatively small set of firms, and some contract terms of interest are used relatively infrequently across firms, or are present to a more pronounced degree in the contracts of one or only a few firms, reporting on these contract features with numerical specificity might permit a reader with specialized knowledge about one or a few firms to infer which firm or firms' contracts were being discussed.

2. General Contract Features

Broadly considered, the contracts observed were similar, regardless of the specific pairings of sellers and buyers, the type of debt involved, and whether the contracts were for "spot" portfolio sales or for a series of forward flow portfolio sales.[3] We nonetheless observed many distinct styles of contracts within the submission of each respondent debt buyer, even when the type of debt being sold was the same in each contract. That is, no "in-house" contractual style uniquely associated with each debt buyer was observed. We also observed, however, that certain contracts were virtually identical (save for particulars of price, quantities, dates, etc.) *across* debt buyers. In some debt buyers' submissions, the names of debt sellers had not been redacted from these contracts, and we observed that a given debt seller wrote virtually identical contracts with different debt buyers. In some instances we were able to identify the original credit issuer of debts being resold from one debt buyer to another, and observed that the terms and conditions in the resale contract tracked the terms and conditions in the credit issuer's contracts. The contracts submission therefore suggests that many of the terms and conditions governing the sale of consumer debts may largely be set by credit issuers.[4]

---

[3] Under forward-flow contracts, debt accounts with specified attributes are sold at regular intervals (typically monthly) at a common unit price negotiated between the buyer and the seller at the outset of the contract. Forward flow contracts typically include termination clauses which permit either party to refuse to make the remaining exchanges under the contract, for cause, without being held to have breached the contract. Termination clauses are generally triggered by specific failures to perform, and not by prevailing market conditions. Each party to a forward flow contract bears a risk that price changes in the "spot" market will move in an adverse manner, such that the locked-in forward flow price becomes disadvantageous relative to the prevailing spot price. When spot market prices change dramatically, relative to the forward flow price, the disadvantaged party may find it more profitable to breach the contract (and risk the payment of damages) rather than to purchase (or sell) the portfolio(s) at the previously agreed-to forward flow price. See, for example, *Chase Bank USA, N.A. v. Unifund Portfolio A LLC*, No. 09 Civ. 9795, 2010 WL 3565169 (S.D.N.Y. Sept. 13, 2010), concerning Unifund's refusal to purchase the July 2008 monthly portfolio under a forward flow contract, entered into with Chase Bank on January 1, 2008, as a result of a large decline in spot market prices relative to what had been prevailing at the time the contract had been signed.

[4] The majority of selling parties in the contracts submitted for this study were credit issuers. In some contracts, intermediaries sold debts on behalf of credit issuers. In other instances, entities that had previously purchased the debts were reselling them to our surveyed firms, sometimes after having made collection efforts on the debt accounts. Contracts where the seller was a credit issuer typically included terms and conditions that specified contractual terms for any subsequent resale of the debts. Both the purchase contracts analyzed in this section, and

All contracts were similar in the sense that they all addressed:

- what type of debt accounts were included in the portfolio being sold by the contract
- the purchase price of the portfolio;
- what rights and obligations each party had in connection to the accounts, and to each other, prior to the exchange;
- how and when the sale would occur; and
- what rights and obligations each party had in connection to the accounts, and to each other, following the exchange.

These common contractual features can be delineated as pre-sale, at-sale, and post-sale terms and conditions. Pre-sale and at-sale terms addressed what was to be exchanged between parties, how the exchange was to take place, and some aspects of the conduct of each party prior to the exchange. Post-sale contractual features encompassed many diverse terms and conditions that affected ongoing relations between sellers and buyers, as well as some aspects of the conduct of either or both parties as it related to consumers. The analysis below follows this delineation, and the greater part is devoted to terms and conditions that affected the post-sale environment in which debt buyers engaged in debt collection activities on the purchased accounts.

3. Pre-Sale and At-Sale Contract Features

(a) Identifying the Assets Being Sold

Contracts must identify the assets being sold and the parties to the contract. Some of the submitted contracts identified debts merely as "certain accounts receivable" and redacted the identities of the sellers in ways that made it difficult to infer what types of debt were being sold. The specific types of debt being transacted would have been known, of course, by the parties to the contract.

---

the approximately 70 additional contracts we received where our surveyed debt buyers were sellers of debt, confirm that original credit issuers' requirements for the presence of particular terms and conditions in resale contracts were honored.

Contracts generally referred to a "bid file" and stated that the consumer accounts sold by the contract would not be materially different from those included in the bid file, or that the attributes of the portfolio would not differ materially from those of the bid file.[5] Virtually all contracts stated that the accounts sold were not chosen in a manner that was materially adverse to the buyer.[6] Some forward flow contracts stated that each portfolio sold under the contract would represent a random-sample of the seller's relevant accounts. We observed some contracts which stated that no accounts within the portfolio would have balances below a certain amount, often $100.[7] In a few instances, contracts stated that the percentage (by value) of accounts in the portfolio associated with consumers residing in particular states would not differ from the proportion of such accounts in the bid file.[8] Beyond this, we saw nothing in the contracts to suggest that credit issuers or debt buyers selected portfolios for specific consumer attributes.[9]

---

[5] When "spot" portfolios are being sold, the bid file may represent a random sample of the accounts being sold. When "forward flow" portfolios are being sold, accounts in the bid file are reflective of the seller's past underwriting standards and collection and charge-off practices, such that future portfolios sold pursuant to the forward flow contract are likely to be statistically similar to those in the bid file, providing the seller does not change its practices.

[6] Some contracts identified particular attributes of the past collection practices associated with accounts in the portfolio, such as whether the accounts had ever been placed with third party collection agencies, and, if so, how many different collection agencies had previously attempted to collect on the accounts.

[7] Typically, these contracts further stated that the minimum balance threshold would be met without the inclusion of interest charges or late payment fees.

[8] For example, a few contracts stated the portfolio sold "shall be materially similar to the Accounts set forth in the Bid File" with respect to "the percentage of the aggregate Unpaid Balance of Accounts for which the primary Borrower's address as reflected in the Sale File is in the states of Florida, Pennsylvania and Texas." A few other contracts contained similar language, but referred to the states of California, Florida, Texas, New York, and Illinois. None of these contracts, however, revealed what the percentage of such accounts had been in the related bid files. We cannot determine, therefore, whether portfolios were being constructed to include few or many accounts from consumers in these states. While specifying the proportion of accounts in a portfolio that related to consumers residing in particular states could be consistent with "forum shopping," it could also be consistent with debt buyer preferences based on state or local licensing laws, laws pertaining to statutes of limitations or other laws affecting collections, a debt buyer's distribution of staff or regional offices, or even with respect to local economic conditions that could affect the probability of successful collections. ("Forum shopping" in a debt buying context refers to the notion that debt buyers select portfolios on the basis of jurisdictions in which collection suits against consumers may be more easily brought and won.)

[9] For example, we did not find any contracts where particular consumer attributes, such as a credit score (current,

(b) Purchase Price of the Portfolio

Contracts commonly referenced a "Closing File," in essence, a snap-shot of the portfolio of accounts being sold, that was created a very short time, typically no more than a few days, before the sale occurred.[10] The Closing File presented a good-faith estimate of what actual account balances would be on the day the transaction occurred.[11] The purchase price percentage rate agreed to by the parties was applied to the aggregate account balance on the Closing File, resulting in the purchase price of the portfolio. The debt buyer then arranged to convey the purchase price to the debt seller in the manner specified by the contract.

(c) Pre-Sale Information Sharing

Contracts typically included a discussion of information sharing between sellers and buyers that occurred during the bidding process and/or the contract negotiation process. This information sharing can include information about some or all of the consumer accounts to be transferred, as well as proprietary information about each party. Both parties agreed to keep this information confidential. In particular, buyers were prohibited from contacting consumers before the sale occurred.

(d) How and When the Sale Will Occur

Contracts typically specified a time and place for the receipt of the buyer's payment and a subsequent transfer to the buyer of the "Sale File." Contracts indicated that Sale Files included an enumeration of the consumer debt accounts sold and their balances on the day of the sale,

---

past, or changes there-in), age, or occupation were selection criteria for the accounts included in the portfolio.

[10] Some contracts identify the date on which the Closing File is created as the "File Creation Date," while others use "Cut-off Date."

[11] Sellers often stipulated that they would cease collection efforts on the accounts, including recalling accounts that had been placed with contingency collectors, at some specified time prior to the File Creation Date. This helps to assure that the account balances on the sale date will be approximately the same as the account balances on the File Creation Date, but does not guarantee such equivalency.

referred to as the "Sale Date" (sometimes also referred to as the "Transfer Date"), as well as other information about each account and the consumer(s) associated with those accounts. The specific types of information that conveyed at sale (as well as some information that may convey shortly following the sale) was often specified by reference to other files which were electronically delivered to the buyer and which we could not observe.[12]

(e) Adjustments to Complete the Sale

While contracts typically stated that sellers would refrain from active collection attempts on the accounts under consideration for sale in the period immediately prior to the sale, events may nonetheless occur which make the face value of some accounts different on the Sale Date than they were in the Closing File. For example, consumer payments could be made to these accounts as a lagged response to past collection efforts, a past charge to the account could be reversed, or a past payment made to the account by check could be reversed due to insufficient funds in the consumer's account. Accordingly, all contracts addressed the manner in which adjustments would be made to either the purchase price or the number and value of accounts sold if the aggregate face value of accounts in the Closing File did not equal the aggregate face value of accounts in the Sale File.

4. Post-Sale Contract Features

The contract features that most interested us were ones that affected how debt buyers collected upon purchased accounts. These contract features primarily concerned what information debt buyers received about consumer debt accounts, what remedies were available to debt buyers in the event that purchased accounts lacked accurate information or were not as

---

[12] Some contracts, however, included hard copies of exhibits that detailed the specific data fields present in the Sale Files. We observed differences across contracts in terms of the types of data that conveyed with sale, but the hard copy exhibits did not reflect whether each type of data was always delivered for each account.

represented by sellers, what limitations credit issuers placed upon how debt buyers, or their employees and agents, interacted with consumers, and whether and how debt buyers could resell purchased debt accounts. These features are examined below.

(a) Quality and Quantity of Account-level Information

The act of extending consumer credit creates records that contain information about consumer debtors.[13] Debt buyers are largely dependent upon credit issuers for the provision of information required to identify consumers and the amounts consumers owe on the debts they purchase.[14] Some of the information debt buyers receive from debt sellers is acquired immediately post-sale, and other information is provided on an as-needed basis at the debt buyers' request.

i. Account Information Provided Immediately Post-Sale

All debt sales contracts provided some account level data immediately post-sale, but different contracts specified different types of data to be provided. Some contracts specified a relatively narrow set of account data, such as the consumer's name, SSN, some contact information, account number, and the account balance. Other contracts specified a broader set of information that may have included additional contact information, including that of a co-debtor, as well as information on the date and amount of the last payment the consumer made on the account and the date and amount of the last purchase made on the account.

Contracts revealed that both sellers and buyers knew that some accounts included within a portfolio might have incomplete or inaccurate data, including data on important information

---

[13] Some consumer information that enters credit issuers' records at the time credit is first extended may, of course, become outdated with the passage of time.

[14] Debt buyers may also use "skip tracers," credit bureaus, and other third-party sources to obtain information about the consumers whose debts they purchase.

such as the then-current balances on accounts. In some instances, debt buyers may have been able to acquire, at a later date, particular pieces of account level data that were missing at the time of sale. In other instances, data missing from the account records at the time of sale may not have been recoverable. There was generally no post-purchase remedy available to buyers when accounts had missing or inaccurate data.

Examples of contract language attesting to the mutual understanding between sellers and buyers that debt account information may be inaccurate or incomplete, and that buyers may be without recourse against sellers when that was the case, included the following:[15]

> "Buyer acknowledges, understands and agrees (i) that Seller makes no representations or warranties whatsoever, express or implied, as to the accuracy of the Current Balance ...." (spot resale of automotive loans)

> "Buyer shall have no right, whatsoever, to make any claim against Seller should the actual unpaid balance of any Loan be different from the Current Balance of such Loan set forth in the Loan Schedule delivered to the Buyer in connection with the sale of such Loan." (spot sale of credit card accounts)

> "Buyer acknowledges and agrees ... Bank has not and does not represent, warrant or covenant the nature, accuracy, completeness, enforceability or validity of any of the Accounts and supporting documentation provided by Bank to Buyer, and, subject to the terms of this Agreement, all documentation, information, analysis and/or correspondence, if any, which is or may be sold, transferred, assigned and conveyed to Buyer with respect to any and all Accounts is sold, transferred, assigned, and conveyed to Buyer on an AS IS, WHERE IS basis, WITH ALL FAULTS." (original emphasis) (spot sale of bank accounts and receivables)

> "Except as stated elsewhere in this Agreement, the Purchased Accounts are sold "as is", and without warranty of any kind, express or implied regarding the Purchased Accounts (including, without limitation, warranties pertaining to validity, collectability, accuracy, sufficiency of information. SELLER expressly disclaims any implied warranties of merchantability or fitness for a particular purpose." (spot sale of telecom accounts)

---

[15] To protect the confidentiality of our respondents' data, we are unable to provide specific citations to contracts. Contract excerpts quoted throughout this section often appear in numerous contracts, and only a few suggestive citations, indicating the type of contract (forward flow or spot), the type of debt sold, and the designation "resale" if the seller is not also the credit issuer, are used.

Very rarely, however, contracts included clauses such as the following:

> "SELLER represents and warrants that each Account is enforceable for its full principal balance … and is the legal, valid, and binding obligation of the maker thereof" (spot sale of "unsecured consumer credit card accounts and related receivables, contract rights and assets")

ii. Additional Account Information That May be Requested by the Buyer

Debt buyers may sometimes wish to obtain copies of account documents created when credit was issued or in connection with the credit issuer's servicing of accounts.[16] Information found in these documents may help debt buyers improve collection efforts and/or investigate consumer disputes.[17] These documents may also be required in connection with court filings when debt buyers sue consumers.

The submitted contracts indicated that account documents typically remained the property of the issuing creditor after the accounts were sold.[18] Because these documents did not convey with the sale of accounts, contracts discussed how debt buyers could obtain document copies from the credit issuer, and contracts differed in the ease and cost with which debt buyers could do so.

A few contracts gave debt buyers free and relatively unrestricted electronic access to account documents for a brief period following the portfolio sale.[19] We observed one contract

---

[16] These documents may include credit applications, account statements, payment records, etc.

[17] Many contracts indicated that sellers either would not orally provide information from these documents to buyers, or indicated hourly charges that buyers had to pay if they requested that such information be provided to them. For example, "Sellers will not be obligated to furnish Buyer with any oral information. If Buyer requests oral information and Sellers have information that Sellers elect to provide, Buyer will pay the hourly rate of $50 for the time and effort in collecting and communicating to Buyer the information requested." (spot sale of credit card accounts) However, one of the debt buyer firms surveyed for this study indicated in its narrative response that its "Account Level Questions" were routinely answered by debt sellers at no charge to the debt buyer.

[18] A few contracts (generally spot sales of telecom debt) indicated that some documents conveyed with the accounts sold.

[19] The quantity of electronic account documents the debt buyer could access was generally limited only by the

with different purchase price percentage rates for accounts depending upon whether digitized account documents were, or were not, available for the accounts. The price per dollar of debt face value for accounts that came with digitized media was $0.061, and $0.059 for accounts without digitized media. Based on the average face value of accounts within the portfolio, this means that accounts with digitized media sold for about $10.50 more than accounts without digitized media. Additionally, we observed a few forward flow contracts for credit card debts which indicated that the seller would "deliver or cause to be delivered to Purchaser for the Accounts to be sold an electronic file, that will contain the Account Documents reasonably available to Seller, within thirty (30) days after each Closing Date, at a cost to Purchaser of five hundred dollars ($500) per monthly purchase file."[20] All of the contracts providing for electronic access to account documents were ones in which the seller was also the credit issuer, and the electronic access was limited to the original debt buyer.

Contracts typically stated that credit issuers would provide a specified number of free document copies to the initial debt buyer, at the debt buyer's request, for a specified period of time. Subsequent purchasers of the consumer debt accounts were generally prohibited from directly contacting the credit issuer for document copies. They were required instead to make such requests through the initial debt buyer, who would then contact the credit issuer and request document copies. Typically, the number of free documents was set equal to a given percentage of the number of consumer debt accounts sold, provided those copies were requested during the

---

number of such documents the credit issuer had available in electronic form. Access was, of course, password-protected and limited to documents related to the accounts purchased by the debt buyer.

[20] A few other contracts stated that some document copies would be delivered electronically, but these contracts generally provided electronic copies on similar payment terms as other contracts which discussed the provision of hard copies of documents.

specified time period.[21] Most often, contracts indicated that copies equal in number to 10% to 25% of the number of consumer debt accounts sold would be provided, for free, during the specified "free period," which was typically anywhere between six months and three years.[22] Credit issuers usually indicated that documents would be provided within 30 to 60 days of their receipt of a written request for documents.

Fees charged after the free time period expired, or when the free quantity limit had been surpassed during the free time period, were typically $5 - $10 per document, but a few contracts set much higher per document fees.[23] Some contracts had tiered document fees which escalated with the passage of time or the aggregate volume of documents requested. Any fees for postage or courier delivery were always the responsibility of the debt buyer.

Many contracts imposed restrictions on how frequently documents could be requested, regardless of whether the documents were being provided for free or for a fee. These restrictions often took the form of limiting how many documents could be requested in any given time period, and/or gave the credit issuer extra time to provide documents when large numbers of documents were requested.[24]

---

[21] Some contracts, however, specified that copies of documents, apparently unrestricted in number, would be provided for a specified percentage of all accounts sold.

[22] Some contracts, however, stated that copies of available account documents would be provided for a given percentage of accounts, without regard to how many documents were requested per account. If debt buyers requested only one document per account, there is no difference between free provision of documents for, say, 10% of accounts and for a number of documents equal to 10% of accounts. The two styles of contractual clauses could have different implications, however, when debt buyers wished to obtain more than one document per account. For example, assume that a contract sets the number of freely provided copies of account documents at 10% of the number of accounts sold. If debt buyers requested copies of two documents per account (say, the application and the last billing statement), then the ceiling on receipt of free document copies would be reached once debt buyers had requested copies for 5% of accounts (two copies per account multiplied by 5% of accounts yields a number of copies equal to 10% of accounts).

[23] Fees of up to $50 per document copy were observed. Some contracts for auto loan, telecommunications, and health club debt, however, did not charge for the post-sale provision of account documents, perhaps suggesting that relatively few documents were available and/or that documents were available electronically.

[24] For example, some contracts stated that: no more than 50 documents could be requested per day; document

Many contracts specified a date beyond which the credit issuer was no longer obligated to provide any account documents to the debt buyer. This date was often set at two to three years following the date of sale.[25]

Notwithstanding the detailed terms and conditions governing access to account level documents, most contracts disclosed that account documents may be unavailable, and that sellers were not required to go to great lengths to produce documents.[26] Some typical clauses included:

> "Buyer understands that some Account Documents may not be available with respect to the Accounts and has taken such lack of available documents into account in determining whether, and at what price, to purchase the Accounts." (forward flow sale of credit card accounts)

> "To the extent Account Documents are available, Seller agrees to use reasonable efforts to deliver Buyer copies of Account Documents ...." (forward flow sale of credit card accounts)

> "For two (2) years after the Closing Date, with respect to Accounts sold on such Closing Date, Seller agrees to provide Buyer with copies (but only to the extent such material may exist, which extent is not guaranteed, warranted or represented) of ... (certain account documents) ... Buyer has been advised by Seller that (a) it is Seller's policy not to retain Account Documents and (b) some of the Accounts do not have an original application or a copy thereof (whether by microfilm, microfiche or other media). To what extent applications are or are not available, is not known by Seller nor represented to Buyer." (spot sale of charged-off credit card accounts)

---

requests, per month, could be no more than 2.5% of the number of accounts sold; requests could not be made more than once per 30 day period; documents for no more than 8% of the total number of accounts purchased could be requested within any 30 day period; or that requests could not be made more than once per 90 day period.

[25] A few contracts, however, indicated that documents might still be provided at later dates if the documents were required for non-collection-related litigation or for collection-related litigation where the document request was made while the accounts were within the statute of limitations.

[26] ACA International has stated that "collectors can have a difficult time providing documentation responsive to the consumer's dispute because creditors may not maintain the appropriate documentation to verify the debt during the collection process" (*The Path Forward: ACA International's Blueprint for Modernizing America's Consumer Debt Collection System*, April 2011, p. 7). Publicly traded debt buyers have stated in their 10-K reports that certain documents may be unavailable from debt sellers, and that the lack of availability may adversely affect their ability to recover on debts. See, for example, Portfolio Recovery Associates' 10-K for the year ended 12/31/09, at p. 18 ("We may be unable to obtain account documents for some of the accounts that we purchase. Our inability to provide account documents may negatively impact the liquidation rate on such accounts that are subject to judicial collections, or located in states in which, by law, no collection activity may proceed without account documents.").

"Documents are to be provided as soon as practicable after requested by Buyer, but all such documentation is provided on an "as available" basis and shall be delivered to Buyer no more frequently than one time per month." (spot sale of loan accounts)

"Nothing ... shall create an obligation on the part of Seller to maintain any current servicing relationships or system of record, and ... Buyer understands that at any time following three years after each Closing Date Seller may cease having the ability to obtain any Account Document using commercially reasonable efforts." (forward flow sale of credit card accounts)

"Seller makes no guarantees as to the availability of applications, statements, records or copies of previous payment checks on any account." (spot resale of "debt receivables")

"Sellers will use commercially reasonable efforts to obtain from prior owners and/or the credit originator directly any Account Documents that Buyer requests and which Sellers are entitled to obtain, at Buyer's sole expense which will be equal to the actual out of pocket costs incurred by Sellers in obtaining the Account Documents." (spot sale of "bank accounts and receivables")

"There is no assurance that any Account Documents will be available. To the extent that Account Documents are reasonably available to Seller, Seller will provide, at Buyer's request, Account Documents for Accounts which total up to 12% of the number of Accounts sold hereunder, at a charge to Buyer equal to Seller's costs payable to the Original Seller for such Account Documents plus 10%." (spot resale of credit card accounts dismissed from Chapter 13 bankruptcies)

"'Account Documents' means, to the extent available or accessible on a commercially reasonable basis to Seller, any credit application, agreement, billing statement, UCC financing statement, notice, correspondence or other document in Seller's possession or accessible on a commercially reasonable basis to Seller which relates to an Account." (spot sale of "unsecured consumer or small business charge or credit card accounts")

"Nothing … shall create an obligation on the part of Seller to maintain any current servicing relationships or system of record, and without limiting any other provisions … Buyer understands that at any time following three years after each Closing Date Seller may cease having the ability to obtain any Account Document using commercially reasonable efforts." (forward flow sale of credit card accounts)

Contracts also indicated that account documents, when available, may be inaccurate and that the provision of account documents could not be relied upon to establish the outstanding balance of an account or that the account represented a valid and collectible debt. Some contracts further stated that missing account documents could be material to the buyer. For example:

> "The Purchaser acknowledges that Seller does not represent, warrant or insure the accuracy or completeness of any information or its sources of information contained in the information provided or in any of the Account Files." (forward flow sale of credit card accounts; spot resale of bank card accounts; forward flow resale of "debt receivables")

> "The existence of Account Documents shall not be deemed to imply that the debt evidenced by the Account Documents is enforceable." (spot resale of credit card accounts)

> "Buyer acknowledges and agrees ... Bank has not and does not represent, warrant or covenant the nature, accuracy, completeness, enforceability or validity of any of the Accounts and supporting documentation provided by Bank to Buyer, and, subject to the terms of this Agreement, all documentation, information, analysis and/or correspondence, if any, which is or may be sold, transferred, assigned and conveyed to Buyer with respect to any and all Accounts is sold, transferred, assigned, and conveyed to Buyer on an AS IS, WHERE IS basis, WITH ALL FAULTS." (original emphasis) (numerous spot sales of bank receivables; numerous spot resales of various consumer debts, including private label credit card accounts)

> "FINALLY, BUYER SHALL BE DEEMED TO UNDERSTAND THAT ANY DOCUMENTS EXCLUDED FROM THE INFORMATION PROVIDED TO BUYER COULD CONTAIN INFORMATION WHICH, IF KNOWN TO BUYER, COULD HAVE A MATERIAL IMPACT ON ITS DETERMINATION OF VALUE OF THE LOANS." (original emphasis) (spot sale of credit card accounts)

Contracts further disclosed that the lack of account documents, or inaccuracies in those documents, would not be considered a breach of the contract, and that the debt buyer had no right of action against the debt seller for unavailable or inaccurate documents. Contracts routinely indicated that sellers would provide affidavits when account documents were unavailable, and indicated that those affidavits would generally attest to the existence of a consumer debt account, its chain of ownership, and the balance on those accounts in the seller's records on the date of sale.

Most contracts provided for affidavits on the same cost and delivery terms as account documents, but often indicated that the maximum number of affidavits that would be provided was below the maximum number of document copies that would be provided.[27] A few contracts charged more for affidavits than for account documents, but pledged to provide affidavits more rapidly.

(b) Post-Sale Remedies for the Purchase of Ineligible Accounts

Contracts defined limited circumstances under which debt buyers could return to debt sellers some of the accounts acquired in a portfolio purchase.[28] When these defined circumstances were met, the accounts were typically called "Ineligible Accounts," "Non-conforming Accounts," "Unenforceable Accounts," or "Impaired Receivables," because they did not conform to certain representations made by the seller.

Contracts typically defined ineligible accounts to include ones where consumers or accounts had a status (*e.g.*, deceased,[29] in bankruptcy,[30] judgment or arbitration award) other than

---

[27] For example, one contracted stated "The Bank will provide a total number of affidavits equal to three percent (3%) of the total Accounts purchased. The Buyer shall be limited to one request for affidavits per week with a maximum of 100 Accounts per request. Bank shall have three (3) weeks to complete the affidavits requested. Requests shall contain sufficient information about the relevant accounts to allow Bank representatives to locate the Account information to complete the affidavits. The Buyer shall pay Bank $10.00 per affidavit requested and provided." (spot sale of credit card accounts) The same contract provided for copies of account documents, when such documents were available, for free, for up to ten percent of all accounts purchased, provided that requests were made within 180 days following the sale. After the number of documents requested exceeded ten percent of the number of accounts sold, or were requested more than 180 days post-sale, the bank charged $10 per document copy requested, and the contract did not indicate an upper bound on the number of document copies that would be provided at that price.

[28] Contracts also specified certain conditions under which the sellers had the right to require the buyer to return certain purchased accounts. These "recall" (or "call back") rights typically centered around the resolution of certain circumstances, such as a pending or threatened suit, action, arbitration or other legal proceeding or investigation relating to the seller, often in connection with specific consumer debt accounts, that are best handled if the seller owns the account(s) in question. The few real estate related contracts observed in the submission contained sellers' call back rights, but did not provide any put-back rights for the buyer.

[29] Contracts differed in whether the death of just the primary account holder was sufficient grounds for a put-back, or whether all account holders had to be deceased, but all required that the triggering death occurred prior to the sale of the account.

[30] Contracts generally permitted put-backs when the primary accountholder had voluntarily filed for bankruptcy, was involuntarily subjected to bankruptcy proceedings, or was in bankruptcy proceedings that had not yet resulted in dismissal or discharge of debts, and these events predated the sale of the account.

the consumer/account status specified in the contract, or where the account resulted from fraud.[31]

Contracts typically indicated that sellers did not intend to sell, and buyers did not intend to

purchase, such accounts.[32] Because these accounts were unintentionally included in the portfolio

of debt accounts, buyers were permitted to "put back" these ineligible accounts to sellers and

receive either a refund or a substantially similar, but eligible, account.[33]

Contracts generally required buyers to determine which accounts were ineligible accounts

within specified time periods, often 180 days post-sale, in order to exercise their contractual "put

back" rights.

The evidentiary standard debt buyers were required to meet to prove that accounts were

ineligible accounts varied across contracts, and some contracts imposed standards which

appeared to be time-consuming or costly to meet.

For put-backs related to ineligibility defined by the consumer's death or bankruptcy filing

prior to the date of sale, the evidentiary standard often appeared to be relatively easy for debt

---

[31] Many contracts used only the term "fraud" and did not specifically mention "identity theft." Contracts also differed in the documentary evidence required to put back accounts due to fraud, and whether the documentary evidence must indicate that the fraud was detected by the consumer prior to the sale of the account.

[32] At other times, however, debt sellers may wish to sell (and debt buyers may wish to purchase) portfolios comprised exclusively of accounts that have been discharged in Chapter 13 bankruptcies (i.e., where the court has imposed a specific repayment plan upon the consumer that the consumer's creditors must accept) or ones that have been dismissed from bankruptcy proceedings (i.e., where the court affords no bankruptcy protection to those debts; most of these accounts would, however, have been shielded from collection activity between the time that consumers sought bankruptcy protection and the time the court dismissed the debts). Contracts for such portfolios were found in the submissions we received, and, in these contracts, an account was ineligible if it was an "ordinary" delinquent account, and not one that had either been discharged or dismissed from bankruptcy. Apart from the definitions used for ineligible accounts, bankruptcy contracts (and contracts with other types of "special status") were very similar to contracts for "ordinary" charge-off consumer debt accounts and we may, without loss of generality, discuss contracts as if they pertained only to charge-off portfolios.

[33] Other circumstances that some (but not all) contracts used to define ineligibility included: the accounts had already been paid in full; the accounts were duplicates of other accounts previously sold; the pre-charge-off principal balance was less than or equal to $25 or the account had a current total balance less than or equal to $300; the accounts had previously been placed with a post-charge-off recoveries agency; the accounts were flagged as "do not work;" and when accounts had previously been included in certain test programs of Seller.

buyers to meet. Some contracts required only "reasonable documentation" or "commercially reasonable written documentation" to support a debt buyer's claim that accounts were ineligible due to consumer death or bankruptcy. Other contracts had more specific put-back documentation standards for death or bankruptcy, such as Lexis/Nexis, Banko, Inc., or consumer credit reports indicating that a consumer was deceased or in bankruptcy.[34] Still other contracts, however, provided specific forms that the debt buyer had to use to document a death/bankruptcy put-back request, and these forms often required copies of death certificates or certified copies of bankruptcy petitions, case numbers, filing dates, and the name and contact information of the debtor's bankruptcy counsel.[35]

Documentation standards for put-backs due to account fraud appeared to be more difficult for debt buyers to satisfy. For example, many contracts, particularly those for charged-off credit card accounts, required documentation that debt buyers could only have obtained from consumers. Some contracts required a copy of a police report and the consumer's Affidavit of Forgery to document a fraud-related put-back request. Other contracts accepted notarized consumer affidavits attesting to fraud, but these affidavits had to be accompanied by copies of

---

[34] The relative ease with which debt buyers may obtain documentation that a consumer is in bankruptcy likely explains why some contracts provide a separate, shorter time period for bankruptcy put backs.

[35] The submission contains numerous contracts between a particular large national bank and several of the surveyed debt buyers for the sale of credit card accounts. These contracts provide very specific and detailed documentary requirements for the reimbursement of ineligible accounts, as follows: "Bankruptcy – Chapter and Date filed and Docket No. and Joint or Individual Filing and Attorney Name and Telephone Number and Court District Name – Bankruptcy filing date must be on or prior to the File Creation Date. If the bankruptcy is an individual filing and the Account is a joint Account, the Account will not be repurchased unless both Cardholders have filed; Deceased – Copy of death certificate or Letter from attorney indicating date of death or Verification from Department of Social Security indicating date of death or Copy of credit bureau indicating date of death or Copy of Obituary – Date of death must be on or prior to the File Creation Date or the Account will not be repurchased. If a joint Account, both Cardholders must have died on or prior to the File Creation Date; Fraud or Dispute Claims – Letter from debtor or debtor's attorney alleging fraud received by (Seller) on or prior to the File Creation Date, which allegation has not been resolved to the Seller's satisfaction by the File Creation Date, Letter from debtor or debtor's attorney alleging a dispute received by (Seller) on or prior to the File Creation Date, which allegation has not been resolved to the Seller's satisfaction by the File Creation Date. Previously Settled – Letter from either the Seller or Collection Agency stating the Account was settled." (original emphasis)

consumers' drivers' licenses or social security cards and police reports of the frauds. A few contracts had less stringent documentation requirements but offered only a 90 day put-back window.

Some contracts further limited fraud-related put-backs only to instances where consumers asserted the fraudulent creation of the debt in a manner which left a specific paper trail *before* the debt was sold, leaving debt buyers without a repurchase remedy for fraudulently created accounts which were not detected (or acted upon) by consumers until after the debt's sale.[36]

Another commonly permissible reason for putting back accounts was that the account had been previously settled by the seller or credit issuer. Here, too, proving to the seller's satisfaction that the seller (or credit issuer) had already settled the debt appeared to be burdensome to the debt buyer. For example, some contracts required copies of a bank or bank-agent letter verifying the settlement, as well as a copy of the canceled check (front and back) by which the settlement payment was made.

Some contracts placed limits on the percentage of accounts that would be accepted as put-backs, stating, for example:

> "Ineligible Accounts submitted for reassignment or refund … may exceed twenty percent (20%) of the total remaining balance purchased; however refund will only apply up to 20% of the total remaining balance purchased. *Buyer will retain ownership of any rejected returns and/or those over 20%.*" (emphasis added) (spot resale of credit card accounts)

> "Seller shall not be responsible for replacing or repurchasing the first five (5%) percent of accounts submitted by Buyer for repurchase or replacement." (spot sale of "credit card and credit line receivables")

> Contracts generally stated that reimbursement for put-back accounts may take 60 days to

---

[36] A few contracts, however, accept the debtor's assertion "in writing that such Account or any transaction on such Account was fraudulently originated or used, which allegation was not resolved to Seller's reasonable satisfaction" as long as the debtor's claim is made no more than 90 days from the closing date.

reach the debt buyer.

All contracts limited the refund debt buyers received for put-back accounts to no more than the account's contribution to the portfolio purchase price. Most contracts permitted debt buyers to keep payments they had received from consumers on accounts that were subsequently put-back to the debt seller, and made adjustments to the repurchase price accordingly. Some contracts required debt buyers to forward consumer payments received on put-back accounts to the debt seller. No contracts discussed returning to consumers the payments they had made on ineligible accounts.

(c) Interactions with Consumers

Contracts typically included some conditions affecting each party's post-sale interactions with consumers. These conditions chiefly affected how consumers were notified about the sale of their accounts, how each party communicated with consumers about the other party, and how payments and consumer correspondence received by the debt seller after the sale would be forwarded to the debt buyer.

i. Notifying Consumers That Their Accounts Have Been Sold

No contracts imposed obligations upon sellers to notify consumers that their accounts have been sold. Some contracts indicated that sellers could, at their option, inform consumers that their accounts had been sold.[37] A few contracts required the seller to refer consumer inquiries to the debt buyer for a specified period of time following the sale.[38]

---

[37] For example, some contracts stated "Seller may, but is not obligated to, give any Borrower written or oral notice of the transfer of the Borrower's Account to Buyer" (forward flow sale of credit card accounts) or "Seller shall have the right, but not the obligation, to mail its own notice addressed to any Obligor at the address shown in its records, notifying such Obligor of the transfer of any Asset or the servicing of the Asset from Seller to Buyer." (spot sale of credit card accounts) These clauses likely protect the seller from violating confidentiality clauses in the contract that would otherwise prevent the seller from discussing the sale with third parties.

[38] For example, a few contracts state "Seller agrees that for a period of two years following the Closing Date, Seller will refer inquiring Customers to the telephone number and address provided by Buyer" or "If Seller is contacted

Most contracts prohibited debt buyers from providing consumers with contact information for the debt seller or credit issuer, even in response to in-bound calls or letters from consumers. An example of fairly typical language used in this regard is the following:

> "Purchaser agrees not to refer any inquiries from a Debtor whose Account was purchased by Purchaser pursuant to this Agreement to Seller, but to handle any such inquiries directly with Seller." (spot resale of credit card debt, also spot sale of installment accounts for consumer goods)

> "The Buyer agrees not to provide the Seller's mailing address, phone number or email address to any Obligor." (spot sale of credit card debt)

Many contracts required debt buyers to notify consumers that their accounts had been sold within a specified period of time, typically 30 to 60 days post-sale. Some contracts required sellers' pre-approval of notices sent by debt buyers to consumers. A few contracts for the sale of freshly charged-off consumer credit card accounts indicated that, for a fee, the selling bank would provide a form letter that the debt buyer could use:

> "At Buyer's reasonable request, the Bank will provide a form letter on an individual basis, at a cost of $10.00 per request, that Buyer may send to a Cardholder to confirm that the Bank sold the Cardholder's Account to Buyer." (both forward flow and spot sales of credit card debts)

Exhibits to these contracts made it clear that the form letter would go out on the debt buyer's letter head, not that of the credit issuer.

Some contracts expressly prohibited debt buyers from using the credit issuer's name in the subject line of notification letters and subsequent collection letters, and limited usage of the seller's name to the body of such letters. Some contracts also required debt buyers to perform a bankruptcy scrub on purchased accounts before contacting consumers, but did not expressly state

---

after the Transfer Date by an Obligor or any person acting on behalf of an Obligor, Seller will direct any such person to contact Buyer by calling … or writing to …." (spot resale of automotive debt)

that debt buyers could not contact consumers identified as being in bankruptcy.[39]

A few contracts relating to portfolios of co-branded credit card debts prohibited debt buyers from referring to the co-branded entities in any written communications to consumers and limited the mention of the co-branded entity to telephonic communications with consumers.

           ii.   Forwarding Payments and Correspondence After Consumer Accounts Have Been Sold

Consumer payments received by previous debt owners following the sale of consumers' debts need to be forwarded to the new owners of those debts. Likewise, correspondence sent by consumers to credit issuers and/or the former owner of their debts, after those debts have been sold, also need to be forwarded to the new owners of those debts.[40]

Contracts differed with respect to how quickly such payments and correspondence were to be forwarded from debt sellers to debt buyers and whether they were forwarded in their entirety. None of the contracts required debt sellers to notify consumers that their payments had been forwarded to debt buyers.[41]

---

[39] Debt buyers may, of their own accord, wish to perform bankruptcy scrubs soon after purchasing accounts, either to assert their put back rights in a timely manner or to avoid contacting consumers who are in bankruptcy. It is not clear why some contracts required debt buyers to do something that may be in their self-interest. A few contracts explicitly stated "Buyer shall immediately cease any collection efforts upon receiving notice (whether from a Cardholder, the Bank, or a third party on behalf of a Cardholder) that a Cardholder has discharged the debt in bankruptcy, and shall not re-commence collection activity until Buyer has conducted a reasonable investigation into the Cardholder's claim and determined, based upon reasonable evidence, that the Cardholder's claim is unfounded." (sale of private label credit card accounts) Bankruptcy scrubs, however, would not fit within the scope of this clause because, while performed by third parties, they are not performed by third parties acting on behalf of debtors. A few other contracts, however, give buyers the option of paying sellers to perform scrubs immediately prior to the sale, so that accounts with deceased or bankrupt consumers can be removed from the portfolio prior to sale: "Prior to Closing, Purchaser Representative will have the right to have each and every Receivable proposed for sale hereunder "scrubbed" for deceased and/or bankruptcy status. Any such procedures will be undertaken at Purchaser Representative's sole expense. Any Receivables qualifying as either a deceased or bankrupt status will be withdrawn by Sellers from the pool of Conveyed Assets rather than treated as an Ineligible Receivable." (spot sale of medical debts)

[40] Consumer correspondence received before a debt was sold would be considered an account document.

[41] Similarly, none of the contracts required debt sellers to forward consumer payments to downstream debt buyers in the event that debts had been resold. Many contracts permitted the resale of debts only upon the prior notice and/or approval of the initial seller. Consequently, many debt sellers would know when debts have been resold, and

Most of the contracts where the debt seller was a depository bank permitted a substantial amount of time, often as much as 60 days, to elapse between the seller's receipt of consumers' payments and the forwarding of those payments to the debt buyer.[42] Most of these contracts also permitted a portion of consumers' payments to be withheld by debt sellers as a service fee after some initial period in which no service fees were charged.[43] These service fees were expressed as either a percentage of the consumer's payment (ranging from 5% to 20%), or as a flat fee (*e.g.*, $5 per payment forwarded). These contracts were generally silent as to when, and in what amount, the debt buyer was required to credit the consumer's account upon receiving delayed, and possibly reduced, consumer payments forwarded from the debt seller.[44] Some of these contracts permitted the debt seller to return the payment to the consumer, rather than forward it to the debt buyer, when payments were received after a contractually specified time; these contracts were silent as to what, if any, explanation the debt seller was required to give the consumer when payments were returned.

Most contracts do not provide a lot of detail about data that accompany consumer account

---

may, therefore, knowingly forward consumer payments to a debt buyer who no longer owns the debt and who then must send the consumer's payment down the ownership chain.

[42] Of course, contracts did not reveal how much time credit issuers, or other debt sellers, actually took to forward consumer payments on to debt buyers, but only the maximum amount of time they could take before violating this term of the contract.

[43] Many of these contracts stated that the seller would charge a service fee for forwarding the consumer's payment, and that the seller could withhold the fee from the forwarded payment. An example of such a clause is: "If payments are received by the Bank from a Cardholder on or after Closing Date, the Bank shall forward such payments (without interest thereon) to Buyer within sixty (60) days from date of receipt. Bank shall charge Buyer a fee of fifteen percent (15%) to process any Account payment received by Bank more than one (1) year after the Closing Date. Bank may, at its discretion, deduct such processing fee when remitting the payments to Buyer." (spot sale of credit card debt)

[44] Unless the full amount of the consumer's payment is credited to the consumer's account, it is the consumer, and not the debt buyer, who is paying the service fee for forwarding the payment. Only a few contracts which imposed service fees for forwarding consumer payments to debt buyers expressly stated that the full amount of the consumer's payment must be credited to the consumer's account. Likewise, only a few contracts expressly stated that the debt buyer must credit the consumer's account as if the debt buyer had received the payment on the same date that the debt seller received the payment (which could be as much as 60 days before the debt buyer received it).

payments forwarded from debt sellers to the debt buyers. A few contracts, however, have

clauses such as the following:

> "Each month after the Closing Date, Bank will forward to Buyer an Account level report detailing all payments Bank has received after the applicable Cut-off Date on the Accounts. Simultaneously, Bank shall wire payment to Buyer or enclose a check for such payments." (spot sale of credit card debt)

> "For a period of four years after the Closing Date, if a Seller receives and collects, after the Cut-Off Date, good funds in payment of any of the Overdraft Balances sold to Purchaser hereunder, Seller will deliver such funds to Purchaser (net of any processing fees due to Seller) … together with information reasonably sufficient to enable Purchaser to credit the same to the appropriate Overdraft Balance." (spot resale of overdraft accounts)

We do not know how account information is transferred when contracts do not include

the atypical specificity used above.

Contracts where the debt seller was a non-depository institution issuing credit cards, or an

issuer of telecommunications, automotive, utility, or medical credit, generally reflected faster

transmission of consumer payments from debt sellers to debt buyers.[45] Service fees for

forwarding payments to debt buyers were also relatively uncommon in contracts for debts other

than credit card accounts. Resale contracts generally passed along the transmittal lags and

service fees inherited from the initial sale contract without substantially adding to either,

regardless of the type of consumer debt being sold.[46]

Many contracts were silent as to the debt seller's responsibility to forward consumer

correspondence to debt buyers. Those contracts that did discuss this, however, generally

---

[45] Many of these contracts stated that payments would be forwarded within 30 days of the sellers' receipt of same, while some said that payments would be forwarded "as promptly as possible," and a few stated that payments would be forwarded within seven to ten days of receipt.

[46] Some of these contracts specified a small turnaround time, others merely stated "as quickly as practical."

indicated that such correspondence would be forwarded relatively quickly, and did not apply any service fee for forwarding correspondence.

(d) The Resale of Consumer Debt Accounts

We observed variation across contracts with respect to restrictions on the resale of debts.[47] Only a few contracts placed no restrictions on the resale of consumer debts, and only a few contracts completely prohibited the resale of consumer debts or prohibited resale during a specified time period.[48] Most contracts required debt buyers to at least notify the seller when debts were resold, and many required the debt buyer to obtain the sellers' consent before reselling debt, although a few contracts required this only for a specified time following the initial debt sale.[49] Some contracts required the debt buyer to receive the seller's consent to both the sale itself and their selection of the party to whom the debts were to be resold, sometimes specifying in detail how debt buyers were to evaluate potential purchasers.[50] Other contracts went beyond this and specifically prohibited the resale of accounts to particular debt buyers

_____

[47] One of our surveyed debt buyers, as a matter of its own business model, did not resell debt during the surveyed period, and so likely would have been indifferent to the debt seller's preferences for contractual terms regarding resales. Another debt buyer indicated that it had decided to stop reselling debt at approximately the end point of our survey period, and its reselling practices could have been winding-down prior to the final cessation. Debt sellers might nonetheless have wanted contracts to reflect their preferences regarding resales as a precaution in case these debt buyers changed their business models in the future and resumed reselling debts.

[48] These contracts generally did, however, permit certain accounts to be resold within the first year following the initial sale if those accounts changed status, *e.g.*, if accounts purchased pursuant to non-bankruptcy portfolios changed status because consumers filed for bankruptcy.

[49] Debt buyers were usually exempted from resale requirements if they were reselling debts to a wholly-owned subsidiary, although some contracts required notice to the seller whenever the buyer sold, pledged, or transferred debts to a wholly-owned subsidiary.

[50] Some other contracts sought to ensure the reputation and reliability of future buyers of resold debts by specifically requiring that "Buyer and all subsequent buyers shall run a Dun & Bradstreet check of all prospective purchasers ("Prospective Purchasers") from Buyer or subsequent buyers of all or part of the Receivables to ensure that no material negative information is reported with respect to such Prospective Purchasers. ... Buyer and all subsequent buyers shall check with the Better Business Bureau to ensure that there is no substantial number of complaints or any material complaints regarding the Prospective Purchaser." (forward flow sale of freshly charged-off credit card debts)

and/or prohibited the resale of debts to particular debt buyers during the first year following the sale.

Contracts generally did not release either party from their obligations to the other party when the original debt buyer resold the accounts.[51] Contracts between debt resellers and downstream debt buyers were required by the original sales contract to repeat many terms and conditions from those original contracts and typically prohibited contact between the downstream debt buyer and the credit issuer.[52] As a result of this, downstream debt buyers who wished to acquire copies of account documents that remained the property of the original creditor were required to make their requests through upstream debt buyers.[53] These same contract features also required that consumer payments and correspondence received by upstream owners (including, but not limited to, the credit issuer) be forwarded downstream, debt buyer by debt buyer, until they reached the owner of the debt.

(e) Possible Consumer Protections Written into Contracts

Some contracts contained unusual features which appeared to protect consumers' interests in how their debts were sold and collected upon.

---

[51] Some examples of language frequently used in contracts between credit issuers and debt buyers in this regard include: "No assignment or transfer of the Agreement or any Loan shall relieve Buyer of any of its liabilities or obligations under this Agreement. Each transferee of this Agreement shall be bound by all of the terms and provisions of this Agreement, and Buyer shall remain liable for all obligations of Buyer to Seller hereunder, notwithstanding such assignment," and "Purchaser agrees that notwithstanding any sale by Purchaser of the Charged-off Accounts purchased pursuant to this Agreement, Purchaser shall continue to be subject to all terms and conditions set forth herein as to charged-off Accounts."

[52] For example, "Any approved third party to whom Purchaser transfers accounts shall not have the right to contact Sellers directly. Purchaser shall remain each Seller's counterpart and any communications between any such approved third-party transferees and each Seller shall go through Purchaser as the intermediary. Sellers shall have the right, but not the obligation, to contact any third-party transferee directly if they receive collection complaints from any Obligor. In such case, Sellers will notify Purchaser of their direct communication with such third-party transferee." (spot sale where three separate bank entities jointly sold of credit card accounts)

[53] A few contracts expressly prohibited a debt buyer from reselling any documents previously acquired from a creditor when reselling debts. Some debt resellers added fees to cover their administrative costs when passing documents up and down the ownership chain.

For example, a few contracts expressly prohibited debt buyers from using any consumer information acquired through the debt sale for the purposes of marketing to consumers and further prohibited debt buyers from selling consumer information to others.[54] Such conditions may follow from the sellers' privacy policies, or could reflect the sellers' desire to retain any value to be derived from marketing to these consumers.[55] Regardless of the sellers' intentions here, contract clauses which prohibit the use or sale of consumer information for any purposes unrelated to the debt buyers' collection efforts may help to protect consumers' privacy.

Some contracts expressly stated that debt buyers would follow all applicable laws and would not add any unauthorized or illegal fees to purchased account balances, and/or provided other clauses to protect consumers from unethical or unlawful collection practices.[56] A few contracts had clauses which indicated that debt buyers must not, in general, attempt to collect upon accounts primarily through litigation, stating, for example, that

> "Purchaser represents and warrants to Seller that Purchaser's primary purpose in purchasing Charged-off Accounts is to attempt legal collection of the Unpaid Balances owed on such Charged-off Accounts and is not to commence an action or proceeding against Cardholders obligated under such Charged-off Accounts." (spot resale of credit card accounts)

A few other contracts had substantially the same clause with "immediately" modifying

---

[54] These clauses are generally of the form "Buyer shall not market to Account Debtors, except for the purposes of collecting a Receivable, or market the names and/or address of Account Debtors." Another variant is "Buyer agrees that any and all demographic data provided by Seller to Buyer pursuant to this Agreement shall only be used by Buyer for purposes of collecting the Debts in the Portfolio. Buyer may not use, sell, transfer or utilize the data for any other purpose without the express written consent of Seller." (spot sales of utility debts, also found in spot sales of medical debts)

[55] For example, some contracts stated "… Sellers shall retain all of the data regarding the Accounts and the Obligors in their or their affiliates' database(s) and shall retain the right to use or license such data for any purposes it may, in its sole discretion, determine." (spot sale of credit card accounts)

[56] For the vast majority of debt buyers, these clauses may be superfluous, as the debt buyers are obligated to adhere to all laws even in the absence of these contractual clauses. Accordingly, the real purpose of these clauses may be to insulate debt sellers from liability or protect them from reputational harm if debt buyers violate the law. Nonetheless, it is possible that these clauses may provide some incremental protection to consumers from unlawful conduct of debt buyers.

"commence." These clauses reflect an effort on the part of the seller to restrain the buyer's use of litigation as a collection method.[57] We lack any evidence on why debt sellers impose these restrictions upon debt buyers. We also lack any evidence on how the debt seller monitors the frequency and/or timing of the debt buyer's collection law suits, or whether debt sellers have ever taken action against debt buyers for breaching these terms.[58]

Nonetheless, if any accounts sold pursuant to these contracts involved wrong consumer/wrong amount claims, consumers may have had more opportunities to resolve these issues if they were shielded from collection law suits filed immediately after the sale of their debts and if the debt buyers to whom their debts were sold did not use collection lawsuits as their primary means of recovering debts.

A few contracts also included clauses that appeared to be designed to prevent debt buyers from attempting to collect from consumers who have previously reported to the seller that the account resulted from identity theft. An example of this type of clause is the following:

> "Prior to initiating any contact, whether verbal, written or electronic, with the Cardholder, Buyer shall … review the portfolio … to discover whether any Accounts included … have indicators, notes or flags that demonstrated that the Cardholder claims to be a victim of identity theft. The Buyer shall immediately notify Bank of any Accounts that have flags or indicators of identity theft and Buyer shall sell the Accounts back to Bank prior to Buyer contacting Cardholders." (spot sale of credit card debts)

A few contracts went further, and required debt buyers to temporarily cease collection attempts and permit the selling bank to investigate if, after the portfolio sale, consumers claimed

---

[57] These contracts were silent, however, as to how a debt buyer's primary purpose was assessed or how "immediately" was defined.

[58] Credit issuers may be concerned that their reputations could be harmed by debt buyers suing substantial numbers of their former customers, or suing former customers very soon after ownership of the debts transferred from the credit-issuer to the debt buyer. Alternatively, credit issuers may be concerned that debt buyers' law suits may "crowd out" legal actions that the credit issuer has taken or anticipates taking by reaching the attachable assets of consumers before the credit issuer can reach them in instances where the same consumer owes debts that the credit issuer retains as well as debts that are sold to the debt buyer.

that debts resulted from unauthorized use or identity theft:

> "Buyer shall immediately cease any collection efforts upon receiving written notice ... that the Cardholder alleges the balance on the Account was the result of unauthorized use or identity theft. Buyer shall not re-commence collection activity on an Account Balance alleged to be the result of unauthorized use or identity theft until (i) Buyer has notified Bank, as soon as commercially practical that the Debtor has alleged that the Account Balance is the result of unauthorized use or identity theft; and (ii) Bank has had an opportunity to investigate the Debtor's allegations. Bank shall, at completion of its investigation, notify Buyer of Bank's review and conclusion. If Bank concludes that Buyer's allegations are supported by the evidence available, Buyer shall not recommence collection action against the Cardholder, and Buyer shall have whatever rights against Bank that Buyer has under ... (the repurchase rights portion of the contract)." (spot sale of credit card debts)

Most other contracts *permitted* debt buyers to put-back accounts that resulted from fraud, but imposed what may be substantial burdens upon debt buyers in doing so.[59] The two contracts excerpted above are unusual in that they *require* debt buyers to sell accounts back to the selling bank when there are indicators of identity theft. The second contract clause excerpted above is particularly unusual in that the seller takes on the cost of investigating whether identity theft occurred, even when consumers first claimed to be victims of identity theft only after the accounts had been sold to the debt buyer. A few other contracts were even more specific as to what the debt buyer needed to do when the consumer stated that the debt being collected on was due to identity theft:

> "When notified by a consumer that their identity has been stolen and they therefore do not owe charges on the account, Purchaser shall in addition to complying with all applicable laws regarding identify theft: (1) Immediately cease any collection activities. (2) Send the consumer the Federal Trade Commission's Theft of Identity Affidavit or similar type affidavit on the same day or next business day that the consumer reports the theft of identity. Upon return of the Theft of Identity Affidavit or similar affidavit, notify in writing within five business days each and every credit bureau to which the collection

---

[59] As discussed above, debt buyers were generally required to obtain copies of documents that were only available from the consumer in order to put back an account due to fraud. Moreover, some contracts further required that the documents must be dated prior to the date of sale, so that the debt buyer was unable to put back an account due to fraud if the consumer did not learn of the fraud in time to leave a paper trail disputing the fraudulent account and/or fraudulent charges dated before the sale occurred.

agency reported negative credit information … The Purchaser shall notify Seller and the consumer in writing within five business days of sending the above letter(s) to the credit bureau(s) … (3) Purchaser agrees to notify Seller and return any Seller account to Seller within five business days if the Purchaser is notified by any credit bureau that the consumer has sent the credit bureau an alert that their identity has been stolen … If the Purchaser has previously reported negative information regarding the Seller account to the credit bureau(s), the Purchaser will request that the credit bureau(s) remove any negative credit information … and promptly notify Seller and the consumer that it has done so …" (spot sale of telecommunications debt)

A few contracts gave sellers rights to monitor debt buyers' collection practices, stating, for example:

"Seller, … shall have the right … to examine and audit records, to include, but not be limited to … records of any disputes and litigation regarding the Receivables, and copies of all letters used in collection of Receivables. In addition, such examination and audit may also include a review of Buyer's collection efforts, cash controls, methods and procedures for recording and remitting payments, and compliance with this Agreement." (spot sale of telecommunications debt)

"From and after the Closing Date, Purchaser agrees … to allow Seller, at Seller's sole cost, to conduct periodic on-site reviews and observations of the Purchaser's collection practices related to the Accounts. Seller shall not be permitted to exercise such inspection right more than two (2) times in any eighteen (18) month period in the absence of any demonstrated misconduct by Purchaser." (spot sale of credit card accounts)

Although these contracts did not state debt sellers' intended use of information gleaned through these inspections, it is possible that their inspection and monitoring of debt buyers' collection practices might protect consumers from collection practices that are unlawful.[60]

Some contracts placed limitations on how debt buyers attempted to collect on out-of-statute debts.[61] Examples of such clauses included

---

[60] A few other contracts contained similar provisions, but also included collection revenue sharing arrangements that were triggered once the debt buyer's collections on the accounts exceeded a certain level. In such contracts, the seller had a self-interest in monitoring the debt buyer's collection practices. The clause cited in the text was not from a contract with a revenue sharing arrangement.

[61] The majority of contracts, however, were either silent as to applicable statutes of limitations or explicitly stated that the buyer had no recourse against the seller if out-of-statute debts were included in the portfolio. A few contracts expressly stated that out-of-statue accounts may be plentiful within the portfolios sold, e.g., "The Sellers believe, but have not verified, that the statute of limitations may have run on some, if not all, of the Accounts." (spot sale of credit card accounts)

"Buyer will not allege with respect to a Receivable any legal rights that do not exist (including representing that a lawsuit will be filed with regard to a Receivable for which the applicable statute of limitations has run)." (spot sale of "certain consumer loan accounts")

and

"If Buyer, or Buyer's assigns or transferees collects or attempts to collect on an Account, Buyer and/or its agent and assigns and transferees will at all times … for any Account where the statute of limitations has run, not falsely represent that a lawsuit will be filed if the Obligor does not pay …" (spot sale of "auto deficiency and/or credit loss accounts")

These clauses may help to prevent default judgments against consumers who did not know that they could assert a statute-of-limitations defense. It also could prevent consumers from unknowingly reviving the statute of limitations by making payments on out-of-statue debts because they feared threatened legal action, though such threats for out-of-statute debts also would violate the FDCPA. Such clauses were typically found in contracts that also included clauses stating that documents would not be provided beyond a specified time following the sale unless the debts were in-statute or the request pertained to litigation unrelated to collection activity.[62] Less commonly, contracts indicated that sellers included out-of-statute debts in their definitions of ineligible accounts. Including out-of-statute debts in the definition of ineligibility permits (but does not require) debt buyers to put-back these accounts upon the seller. When debt buyers put-back out-of-statute debts to debt sellers instead of attempting to collect on those debts, consumers receive the protections offered by the statute of limitations, regardless of whether they know to assert the statute of limitations as a defense against a collections lawsuit, since such suits would not occur, and would not unknowingly revive the statute of limitations by

---

[62] An example of this type of clause is "Except in instances of litigation unrelated to collection activity or accounts that are within the statute of limitations at the time requested, the Bank will have no obligation to provide Buyer with Account Documents after three years from the Closing Date." (spot sale of credit card debt) Note, however, that under such a clause documents requested within three years following the sale would be provided even if the debts were out-of-statute.

making a partial payment.

A few contracts prohibited debt buyers from adding any amount to the account balances purchased from sellers, stating, simply "Purchaser agrees not to add any further interest or fees to the Account Balances." (spot sale of "certain unpaid patient receivables due from patients")

TECHNICAL APPENDIX D: DESCRIBING PORTFOLIO DATA

Technical Appendix D: Describing Portfolio Data

The nine firms surveyed for this study submitted data on 5,053 portfolios.[1] These

portfolios contained nearly 90 million consumer accounts, reflecting nearly $143 billion in

consumer debt (face value). The nine firms spent nearly $6.5 billion to acquire these debts.

Our 6(b) orders, at specification II.A.3.d, asked debt buyers about the types of accounts

in each portfolio they had purchased during the relevant time period ("For each portfolio …

provide … the types of accounts included (*e.g.*, credit card, medical, auto, etc.)"), and did not ask

whether accounts had a special collection status, such as "bankruptcy" or "deceased consumer,"

or whether debts resulted from judgment or arbitration awards.[2]

Seven debt buyers nonetheless revealed that some or all of the portfolios they had

purchased were comprised of debts of consumers who had filed for bankruptcy.[3] Some of these

firms provided us with both bankruptcy status information and type of debt account information,

and some provided bankruptcy status information in lieu of submitting type of debt account

---

[1] This does not include one submitted portfolio comprised entirely of accounts originated by a Brazilian bank to Brazilian consumers.

[2] The status of a debt account may affect the recovery methods used by debt collectors, and thereby affect the amount, cost, and timing of recoveries. For example, bankruptcy law prohibits debt collectors from "dunning" consumers who have filed for bankruptcy protection. *See* 11 U.S.C. § 362(a)(6) (2006) (staying "any act to collect, assess, or recover a claim against the debtor that arose before the commencement of the case" in federal bankruptcy court). Instead, creditors, or debt collectors acting on their behalf, file claims with the bankruptcy court and await the determinations of the court, which may include, in the case of Chapter 13 filings, a repayment plan that can extend over a number of years. *See id.* § 501 (proof of claim); § 1322 (contents of a Chapter 13 plan). When creditors, or debt collectors acting on their behalf, prevail in litigation against consumers, state laws may permit additional methods of recovery, such as garnishing consumers' wages and bank accounts. *See* FED. TRADE COMM'N, REPAIRING A BROKEN SYSTEM: PROTECTING CONSUMERS IN DEBT COLLECTION LITIGATION AND ARBITRATION 5-6 (2010), *available at* http://www.ftc.gov/os/2010/07/debtcollectionreport.pdf. The status of a consumer debt can also affect the statute of limitations governing collections on the debt. Many states stay the statute of limitations on debts in bankruptcy until and unless debts are dismissed from bankruptcy. *See, e.g.*, *Zinchiak v. CIT Small Bus. Lending Corp.*, 406 F.3d 214 (3d Cir. 2005) (interpreting 42 PA. CONS. STAT. § 5535 to toll the Pennsylvania statute of limitations for collection actions while a bankruptcy stay is in place); *Schumacher v. Worcester*, 64 Cal. Rptr. 2d 1 (Ct. App. 1997) (interpreting CAL. CIV. PROC. CODE § 356 to toll the California statute of limitations in such circumstances). In addition, many states have a longer statute of limitations for collections on judgment and arbitration awards than they do for consumer debts for which no judgments have been obtained. *Compare, e.g.*, CAL. CIV. PROC. CODE § 337 (Deering 2012) (four years for written contractual debts in California) *with id.* § 337.5 (ten years for debts supported by judgment); NY C.P.L.R. 213 (Consol. 2012) (six years for contractual debts in New York) *with* NY C.P.L.R. 211 (twenty years for debts supported by judgment).

[3] A few firms additionally revealed that some portfolios contained accounts of deceased consumers or accounts associated with judgment or arbitration awards.

information. Because the 6(b) orders did not ask the debt buyers to identify bankruptcy

portfolios, we cannot be certain whether all of the portfolios not identified as bankruptcy

portfolios were indeed not bankruptcy portfolios, both for firms that identified some bankruptcy

portfolios and the two firms that did not.[4]

The two tables below show various portfolio attributes broken out according to the firms'

self-report of whether or not portfolios were bankruptcy portfolios, and our simplifying

assumption that portfolios not self-reported as bankruptcy portfolios were "charge-off" portfolios

(that is, portfolios of delinquent debt that had been charged-off as uncollectible by the original

creditor and which did not have any special status, such as bankruptcy, deceased debtor, or

arbitration or judgment award).[5]

---

[4] The two firms that did not indicate whether any of the portfolios they purchased were of bankruptcy accounts indicated that they had sold portfolios of bankruptcy debt. This may suggest that they did not maintain the systems required to make recoveries on debts in bankruptcy. Additionally, neither of these firms included any information that would be relevant to the purchase of bankruptcy portfolios (*e.g.*, the bankruptcy case number, the applicable Bankruptcy Code chapter, the bankruptcy petition date, etc.) in their responses to order specification II.B.3, which addressed the information and documents that debt buyers obtained or obtained access to when deciding whether to purchase a portfolio of consumer accounts.

[5] In addition to the possibility that some of the portfolios not identified as bankruptcy portfolios may consist of bankruptcy or other special status accounts (*e.g.*, deceased debtor, arbitration or judgment awards), some portfolios may consist of performing debt. One debt buyer, for example, specifically noted that account charge-off dates were "not applicable" for approximately three dozen of the portfolios it submitted, none of which were among the ones it identified as bankruptcy portfolios. Some contracts submitted for this study, as well as some 10-K reports of publicly-traded debt buyers, indicate that debt buyers occasionally purchase portfolios of performing debt (*i.e.*, debt that was not charged-off as uncollectible by the credit issuer).

Table D1: Basic Characteristics of Submitted Portfolios

Account status at time of purchase	Portfolios		Accounts		Face Values (a)			Acquisition Expenditures (b)		
	#	%	#	%	$	%	Avg. FV of accounts	$	%	per $ of Face Value
Charge-off	3,087	61%	77,675,862	87%	$104,733,044,243	73%	$1,348	$5,014,641,267	78%	$0.04788
Bankruptcy	1,966	39%	11,357,757	13%	$38,194,615,739	27%	$3,363	$1,426,349,243	22%	$0.03734
Total	5,053	100%	89,033,619	100%	$142,927,659,982	100%	$1,605	$6,440,990,510	100%	$0.04506

Table Notes:

(a) Aggregate face values were computed by multiplying the average face value of accounts in each portfolio (as requested at specification II.A.3.g) by the number of accounts in each portfolio (as requested at specification II.A.3.c), and then summing across all relevant portfolios. Average face value figures were calculated by dividing the relevant aggregate face value by the relevant aggregate number of accounts.

(b) Specification II.A.3.e requested the amount paid for each portfolio. Acquisition expenditures per dollar of face value figures were calculated by summing the amount paid for each portfolio across all relevant portfolios and then dividing by the relevant total face value as described in (a), above.

The following table looks at portfolio characteristics within the sub-categories of charge-off and self-reported bankruptcy portfolios.

Table D2: Characteristics of Portfolios Submitted by Nine Debt Buyers

Type of Debt Accounts Within Charge-off Portfolios (a)	Portfolios		Accounts		Face Values (m)		Acquisition Expenditures (n)	
	#	% of All Charge-off Portfolios	#	% of All Charge-off Accounts	% of All Charge-off Portfolios	Avg. Face Value of Accounts	% of Charge-off Portfolios	Per $ of Face Value
Credit Card (b)	1918	62%	35,220,694	45%	65%	$1,943	71%	$0.05224
Medical (c)	530	17%	21,500,329	28%	7%	$345	3%	$0.01909
Consumer Loans (d)	161	5%	1,014,011	1%	4%	$3,785	2%	$0.03219
Utilities	73	2%	1,483,133	2%	1%	$480	0%	$0.01718
Telecomm	68	2%	11,299,647	15%	5%	$438	3%	$0.02983
Mixed (e)	66	2%	2,067,028	3%	6%	$3,026	3%	$0.02595
Auto Loans (f)	59	2%	1,084,058	1%	7%	$6,489	2%	$0.01560
Other (g)	57	2%	2,832,530	4%	2%	$898	2%	$0.03229
"Credit cards & Lines of Credit"(h)	54	2%	276,779	0%	2%	$7,229	3%	$0.06598
Student Loans	52	2%	416,974	1%	0%	$735	0%	$0.03484
Mortgages(i)	35	1%	20,683	0%	1%	$48,669	10%	$0.50442
Overdrafts	8	0%	439,651	1%	0%	$447	0%	$0.05017
Not Stated	4	0%	155	0%	0%	n/a	0%	$0.00094
Bad Checks	2	0%	20,190	0%	0%	$156	0%	$0.01944
Sub-total (j)	3087	100%	77,675,862	100%	100%	$1,348	100%	$0.04788
Type of Bankruptcy Filing Within Bankruptcy Portfolios	#	% of All BK Portfolios	#	% of All BK Accounts	% of All BK Portfolios	Avg. Face Value of Accounts	% of BK Portfolios	Per $ of Face Value
Bankruptcy Portfolios:(k)								
Chp. 13 Bankruptcy (l)	1690	86%	7,977,364	70%	61%	$2,931	99%	$0.06067
Chp. 7 Bankruptcy	276	14%	3,380,393	30%	39%	$4,382	1%	$0.00052
Sub-total	1966	100%	11,357,757	100%	100%	$3,363	100%	$0.03734
Total of All Portfolios	5053		89,033,619			$1,605		$0.04506

Table Notes:

(a) Firms freely designated account descriptors.

(b) "Credit Card" includes general purpose credit cards (often specifically designated as "Visa," "MasterCard," etc.) as well as accounts designated "private label credit card," "subprime credit card," "consumer credit card," and "business credit card." Although we collectively treat these as "credit cards," the distinctions among sub-types may be important to firms. See, for example, Portfolio Recovery Associates' 10-K report for the year ended December 31, 2009, at p. 7, where "major credit cards" are distinguished from "private label credit cards" when listing "Life to Date Purchased Face Value of Defaulted Consumer Receivables."

(c) "Medical" includes accounts designated by some firms as "healthcare." A small percentage of these portfolios were comprised of accounts with very high average face values (e.g., five and even six figure amounts) that suggest large hospital bills. The vast majority of the portfolios, however, were comprised of accounts that had low and mid three figure balances, as reflected by the average face value of accounts calculated for all submitted medical portfolios.

(d) "Consumer Loans" also includes accounts designated as "installment loans," "personal loans," and "unsecured consumer loans."

(e) "Mixed" includes firms' own use of the descriptor "mixed" as well as instances where firms used multiple account descriptors within portfolios (e.g., "credit card, consumer loans, auto," or "credit card, auto, consumer loan, installment loan, telecom," etc.) and we assigned the term "mixed." "Credit cards" were expressly mentioned in "mixed" portfolios more often than any other descriptors (58 portfolios) and "auto" was the second most frequently used descriptor (25 portfolios). Accordingly, the true percentages of all submitted accounts that fell into the categories "credit card" and "auto" exceed the percentages attributed to these categories in the table.

(Table continued on next page.)

Table Notes (continued):

(f)   "Auto Loans" may include loans that are secured by vehicles as well as unsecured loans (*i.e.*, auto loan deficiencies) which result when the value of repossessed autos fall short of the outstanding loan amounts.

(g)   This includes instances where firms self-reported "other" or "misc." as the type of debt, as well as some express but infrequently used debt account descriptors, such as "debt consolidation service."

(h)   Several firms used the express descriptor "credit cards and lines of credit," even though they also report "credit cards." No firms reported portfolios comprised solely of "lines of credit." Because of this, we have opted to break-out "credit cards & lines of credit" as a separate category. While these portfolios could have been placed into the "mixed" category, that would have obscured the fact that "credit cards & lines of credit" portfolios had average face values ($7,229) that were more than twice the average face values of other "mixed" portfolios ($3,026).

(i)   The average expenditure per dollar of face value for mortgage accounts is sensitive to the presence of a small number of mortgage portfolios for which the average acquisition expenditures per dollar of face value was in excess of 75 cents on the dollar; some of these portfolios were expressly linked to contracts for the purchase of performing mortgage loans. In contrast, a significant number of mortgage portfolios had average acquisition expenditures per dollar of face value that were below one cent on the dollar; some of these portfolios were expressly linked to contracts which indicated that the portfolios pertained to properties that had already been foreclosed on and/or for which the consumer had declared bankruptcy. The median acquisition expenditure per dollar of face value for all mortgage portfolios was $0.10000, or ten cents on the dollar.

(j)   Cumulative rounding errors may prevent percentage figures from summing to 100%.

(k)   Five of the seven firms who reported purchases of bankruptcy portfolios also revealed the type of debt within the portfolios; 84% of their bankruptcy portfolios were comprised of credit card debt. These five firms purchased 72% of the 1,966 self-reported bankruptcy portfolios. Accordingly, we estimate that at least 60% of all bankruptcy portfolios are comprised of credit card debt (84% of 72% is 60%).

(l)   Three firms expressly indicated the Bankruptcy Chapter pertaining to their self-reported bankruptcy portfolios. Three other firms indicated in their narrative reports that virtually all of their purchases of bankruptcy portfolios pertained to Chapter 13 filings. One firm used "Paying Bankruptcy" as a descriptor, and we have assumed that to indicate a Chapter 13 bankruptcy.

(m)   To conserve space horizontally, the aggregate face values for each type of debt account have been omitted. Aggregate face values were computed by multiplying the average face value of accounts in each portfolio (as requested at specification II.A.3.g) by the number of accounts in each portfolio (as requested at specification II.A.3.c), and then summing across all portfolios of the same type. Average face value figures were calculated by dividing the relevant aggregate face value by the relevant aggregate number of accounts.

(n)   To conserve space horizontally, the aggregate acquisition expenses for each type of debt account have been omitted. Specification II.A.3.e requested the amount paid for each portfolio. Acquisition expenditures per dollar of face value figures were calculated by summing the amount paid for each portfolio across all portfolios of the same type and then dividing by the relevant total face value as described in (m), above.

Charge-off Portfolios

Portfolios which were not self-reported as bankruptcy portfolios comprised 61% of all portfolios submitted for study, and 78% of expenditures on debt acquisition.[6] By all measures,

---

[6] Accounts can change status after a debt buyer purchases them. Some of the consumers whose accounts were purchased in bankruptcy portfolios may have subsequently had their bankruptcy cases dismissed; following dismissal, their accounts again became collectable in the same manner as any other charge-off accounts. Similarly, consumers whose accounts were purchased in charge-off portfolios may have sought bankruptcy protection following the debt buyers' purchase of their accounts, precluding their accounts from being collectable through regular collection channels. Our data do not specifically track changes in consumers' bankruptcy status during the period covered by our study. We assume, however, that submitted data on collection activities relating to accounts acquired via the purchase of portfolios that firms identified as being bankruptcy portfolios indicate that consumers associated with those accounts have had their bankruptcy petitions dismissed, making their debts collectable.

credit card debt was the leading asset type within portfolios that were not identified by debt buyers as bankruptcy portfolios.

Credit card portfolios accounted for 62% of all submitted portfolios not identified by debt buyers as bankruptcy portfolios; the next highest asset class was medical debt, which comprised 17%. Each other debt category accounted for no more than 5%.

Credit card accounts comprised 45% of all submitted accounts associated with portfolios that were not identified as bankruptcy portfolios. Medical debt accounts and telecommunications debt accounts were the next largest individual debt categories by percentage of accounts purchased, at 28% and 15%, respectively.

The aggregate face value of consumer debts in all submitted portfolios not identified by debt buyers as bankruptcy portfolios exceeded $104 billion. Credit card debts accounted for 65% of this amount. Medical and auto debt each accounted for 7%, "mixed debt" accounted for 6%, and each of the other debt categories accounted for no more than 5%.

Credit card portfolios accounted for an even larger share, 71%, of all expenditures on portfolios that were not self-reported as bankruptcy portfolios. The second largest debt category was mortgage debt, at 10%.[7] Each of the remaining debt categories accounted for, at most, 3% of acquisition expenditures.

Expenditures amounted to an average of 4.8 cents per dollar of face value for portfolios regarded as charge-off portfolios.[8] Expenditures per dollar of face value were highest for mortgage debt, at 50 cents per dollar of face value, and between approximately 1.5 and 6.6 cents

---

[7] As discussed in note (i) of Table D2, some of these portfolios were expressly linked to contracts for the purchase of performing mortgage debt and had very high expenditures per dollar of face value. Other portfolios, for which no contracts were submitted, had similarly high acquisition expenditures per dollar of debt. If both of these categories are excluded from the analysis, the mortgage debt share of total acquisition cost would fall to less than one-half of one percent.

[8] Overall, for all types of debt (both charge-off and bankruptcy), acquisition expenditures amounted to an average of 4.5 cents per dollar of debt face value.

on the dollar for all other types of debt.[9]

Bankruptcy Portfolios

Two of the seven firms that volunteered that they had purchased portfolios of bankruptcy debt indicated that bankruptcy debt was the only type of consumer debt they purchased. These two firms jointly accounted for 62% of all portfolios in the submission that were self-reported as bankruptcy portfolios. These two firms further revealed the underlying type of account (*e.g.*, credit card, medical, auto) in each portfolio of bankruptcy debt they purchased.[10]

Five other firms reported purchasing bankruptcy portfolios. Two of these five firms reported purchasing substantial numbers of bankruptcy debt portfolios, although these portfolios did not form the majority of their purchased debt portfolios.[11] One of these firms further revealed the type of debt accounts in each of its bankruptcy debt portfolios and the other firm did not.[12] Three other firms reported purchasing small numbers of bankruptcy portfolios which comprised very small proportions of their aggregate portfolio purchases.[13] Of these three firms, two expressly revealed the chapter of the U.S. Bankruptcy Code under which consumers had

---

[9] Although the average expenditure per dollar of face value may not be a good indicator of typical expenditure for mortgage portfolios (see note (i) to the table), mortgage debt would still be the most valuable debt, in terms of expenditure per dollar of face value, even if the median value (ten cents of expenditure per dollar of face value) were used in the comparison.

[10] These two firms revealed in their narrative reports that their business models were specialized to the recovery of bankruptcy debts, and the spreadsheet data they submitted on their purchased portfolios provided the "type of account" information requested in specification II.A.3.d of the 6(b) orders. These firms provided information in their narrative reports about the proportions of their purchased portfolios that pertained to particular chapters of the U.S. Bankruptcy Code.

[11] In each instance, however, bankruptcy portfolios accounted for more than 40% of the total number of portfolios purchased by these two firms.

[12] The firm that revealed the type of debt account associated with each of its bankruptcy portfolios did so in responding to specification II.A.3.d of our order, and revealed the chapter of the U.S. Bankruptcy Code under which consumers had sought bankruptcy protection in a narrative response. The other firm responded to specification II.A.3.d by revealing the chapter of the U.S. bankruptcy code under which consumers had sought bankruptcy protection and did not provide any information (even narratively) about the type of debt accounts included in its bankruptcy portfolios.

[13] Combined, these three firms reported less than 10 bankruptcy portfolios.

sought bankruptcy protection.[14] Two of these three firms further revealed the type of accounts (*e.g.*, credit card, medical, auto) in the bankruptcy portfolios in responding to specification II.A.3.d, and the third firm answered II.A.3.d for its bankruptcy portfolios by giving just the chapter of the U.S. Bankruptcy Code under which consumers had sought bankruptcy protection.[15]

Self-reported bankruptcy portfolios comprised 39% of all 5,053 submitted portfolios, but just 22% of all expenditures for portfolio acquisition. The data submitted do not permit us to observe how many self-reported bankruptcy portfolios, or accounts within such portfolios, pertained to secured or unsecured assets. We estimate, however, that at least 60% of all accounts in self-reported bankruptcy portfolios related to credit cards debts (see note (k) in the table above), and therefore assume that the majority of self-reported bankruptcy accounts submitted related to unsecured assets. Eighty-six percent of the portfolios self-identified as bankruptcy portfolios, and 99% of the accounts in portfolios self-identified as bankruptcy portfolios, pertained to Chapter 13 bankruptcy petitions. We were unable to determine, however, the extent to which these portfolios reflected Chapter 13 filings which already had a court-ordered repayment plan in place or were awaiting a determination of whether or not a repayment plan would be instituted.[16]

Expenditures amounted to an average of 3.7 cents per dollar of face value for portfolios regarded as bankruptcy portfolios. The expenditures per dollar of face value differed according to the identified bankruptcy chapter; the figure was much higher for Chapter 13 portfolios than

---

[14] The third firm implied that consumers had sought protection under Chapter 13 and had obtained court-ordered repayment plans by referring to "paying bankruptcies."

[15] In each instance, these three firms supplied this information in their responses to II.A.3.d.

[16] Some creditors may sell the debt accounts very soon after receiving notification that consumers have filed a Chapter 13 bankruptcy petition and before the Court has either authorized a repayment plan or dismissed the consumer's case.

Chapter 7 portfolios, 6.1 cents on the dollar versus 0.05 cents on the dollar, respectively.

Judgment Portfolios

A small number of the seven firms that voluntarily revealed which of their portfolios were of accounts in bankruptcy also voluntarily revealed having purchased a small number of portfolios of judgment accounts.[17] We cannot be certain whether or not the remaining firms also purchased judgment delinquencies. There are several indicators, however, which suggest that the purchase of judgment accounts could be more prevalent than what was expressly and voluntarily revealed in the firms' submissions.[18]

Deceased Debtor Portfolios

None of the nine debt buyers indicated that any of their portfolios were comprised exclusively of the accounts of deceased consumers.[19]

---

[17] Judgment accounts result from unpaid legal judgments against consumers. The contracts submitted by debt buyers that referenced judgment accounts indicated that these judgments pertained to delinquent debts, although other types of unpaid legal judgments are, of course, possible. When consumers are successfully sued over delinquent credit card debts, for example, the amount awarded by the court to the creditor replaces the debt that was the subject of the litigation, and creates a new debt obligation that, typically, commences a new statute of limitations period and may also permit additional collection methods (*e.g.*, garnishment of wages or bank accounts or liens against real property) that may not have been available prior to the judgment. *See* FED. TRADE COMM'N, REPAIRING A BROKEN SYSTEM: PROTECTING CONSUMERS IN DEBT COLLECTION LITIGATION AND ARBITRATION 5-6 (2010), *available at* http://www.ftc.gov/os/2010/07/debtcollectionreport.pdf; 46 AM. JUR. 2D *Judgments* § 458 ("[W]hen a valid final judgment is rendered, the original debt or cause of action, or underlying obligation upon which an adjudication is predicated, merges into the judgment. The original claim is extinguished and a new cause of action on a judgment is substituted for it."); *compare, e.g.*, CAL. CIV. PROC. CODE § 337 (Deering 2012) (four year statute of limitations period for written contractual debts in California) *with id.* § 337.5 (ten years for debts supported by judgment); NY C.P.L.R. 213 (Consol. 2012) (six years for contractual debts in New York) *with* NY C.P.L.R. 211 (twenty years for debts supported by judgment). Our data do not permit us to determine whether any of the judgment accounts submitted to our study resulted from default judgments.

[18] For example, in responding to specification II.D.1 ("Describe the information and documents about a portfolio that the Company obtains or obtains access to from the seller at the time the Company purchases a portfolio.") one firm responded, in part, by describing the types of information obtained on legal judgment accounts (*e.g.*, "For legal judgment accounts, the additional fields might include …"), but did not submit any portfolios that it expressly identified as being comprised of judgment accounts. A few contracts pertain to judgment and arbitration awards, although the firms which submitted these contracts did not voluntarily identify any portfolios as pertaining to judgment or arbitration awards.

[19] A small number of contracts, however, indicated that deceased consumer accounts were included in portfolios that combined accounts with different types of collection status. For example, one contract indicated that a portfolio contained a mixture of bankruptcy, deceased consumer, judgment, out-of-statute, and pre-litigation accounts, but the debt buyer's response to Specification II.A.3.d (type of debt) for the portfolio in question was "credit card," because, presumably, all of the accounts with these various statuses were credit card accounts. No firms that specialize in collecting on deceased accounts were included in the study.

www.ingramcontent.com/pod-product-compliance
Lightning Source LLC
Chambersburg PA
CBHW080811180526
45168CB00006B/2404